MAGIC, MYTH AND MEMORIES
in and around the Peak District

Doug Pickford

Published by Sigma Leisure – an imprint of
Sigma Press, 1 South Oak Lane, Wilmslow, Cheshire SK9 6AR, England.

British Library Cataloguing in Publication Data
A CIP record for this book is available from the British Library.

ISBN: 1-85058-373-0

Typesetting and Design by: Sigma Press, Wilmslow, Cheshire.

Cover design: Martin Mills

Printed by: Manchester Free Press

General Disclaimer

Whilst every effort has been made to ensure that the information given in this book is correct, neither the publisher nor the author accept any responsibility for any inaccuracy.

Preface

There is a Wise Man who lives in the border country of the Three Shires – Cheshire, Derbyshire and Staffordshire. He claims to be able to move clouds in the sky.

He does not call himself Wise Man but others do. He goes about his daily employment in a nearby town and then on his private life away from the rigours of the office environment he helps people, if they should ask. He heals by the laying on of hands or by the transference of healing thoughts, many a time without the sick person knowing this is taking place at that moment. He knows herbs that are beneficial and uses water from a hill spring, fresh, cool and clear, as an aid to recovery from illness. He is also aware of what he terms "the Lie of the Land". This has also been called the Spirit of the Place or the "Right Feeling". It is that knack of instantly realising what has gone before at a hill, a dale, a field, a farm or maybe an ancient stone circle. He is aware of what millions of people used to be aware of and what so many have now lost or perhaps, do not realise they still possess. It is just as much a sense as sight, smell, touch, taste, hearing or balance. It is a common sense that has, alas, become uncommon.

Our predecessors were far more aware of its existence. Not all could utilise it to advantage, just as today not all of us can, for instance, utilise our tastebuds as a wine expert would or our hearing as a piano tuner could. They of the past who could take advantage of this sense of the place would have been able to feel the energy emanating from rocks and the earth; an energy that could be used to heal not just people but livestock as well. They would have sensed a piece of land was good or bad; they could sense what wild animals knew (and still know) about unseen tracks across the landscape; they could sense the beneficial properties of both Sun and Moon, wind and rain, fire and ice.

Today, the vast majority of us have had this realisation of what is about us suppressed. Town and cities have buried a great deal of what the earth offered us and most people who live, through choice or necessity, in an urban environment do not have the opportunity to look at what is still outside the city walls at those green hills far away and what those hills are saying to us if we could only listen. Perhaps when we do get out into the "countryside" some of our senses are too dulled to appreciate the Lie of the Land or the Spirit of the Place but blame for this, if blame there should be, must lie with much that has deliberately taken place over the centuries--the attitude that anything to do with rural or earthly customs and practises is somehow "pagan" and therefore should be stamped upon; most certainly discouraged and, proverbially, swept under the carpet. They used to burn people at the stake for it, you know.

There is still an enormous amount of evidence around and about of what some would term primitive belief or belief that used to be. It is quite abundant, in fact, and if we allow ourselves to discard our blinkers and, in extreme cases, blindfolds, we can see where the clues lie around the land. There are stones that people visit, even today, in order to be healed of afflication; there are stones around which our predecessors lit fires to cleanse both livestock and people (and where there is still evidence of charcoal remaining); there are places where magical events can still occur if they are allowed to and there are spots where our senses may tell us it is not wise to visit.

In the forthcoming chapters of this book we shall see just how much Earth Knowledge has been suppressed and we shall, hopefully, discover quite a bit that is still around us. We'll look at stone circles that have been on our doorsteps, as it were, for thousand of years but have not been identified as such until now; we'll look at the faery folk, delve into a Sacred Grove of the ancients; discover healing properties of mud and stone and, in short, just look at what is there. And while we're at it, there will be some interesting characters popping up like the Arthurian Knight of the Twentieth Century who held Druidic Rites and the dwarf form the Otherworld who steals apples. I have also brought in to the narrative a few less flamboyant characters than these two, but nevertheless, characters who could be termed larger than life or, at the very least, could be termed "interesting". This has been done in an endeavour to bring across the fact that history and geography and tradition would be nothing if not for the people who made history, moulded the geographical features and invented tradition; as well as those who appreciated what the earth can give.

I have compiled this book for a variety of reasons, not least because of encouragement by the great number of good people who contacted me after reading my previous work *Myths and Legends of East Cheshire and the Moorlands* which also goes by the title *A cabinet of curiosities*. In this I hinted at many aspects of earth magic and tradition and must have whetted appetites for more judging by the requests for talks to groups, practical demonstrations of dowsing and healing and the barrage of questions that followed its publication. Also, as a result of that book, I have had the enormous good fortune of meeting some quite amazing people who, as well as becoming (I hope) lifelong friends have demonstrated aspects of the past, present and future I had been unaware of up until then. A number of these fine folk and their talents are mentioned within these pages.

And then, of course, there is my dear wife, Hilary, whose talents as a visionary and a psychic have been of enormous help. She has visited sites with me and seen what was patently obvious; what have been there for centuries upon centuries but never noticed. She has investigated mysteries and unravelled them and it is true to say this book could not have been compiled without her assistance.

So once again the invitation is extended to join with us and explore the curiosities, the mysteries and the unknown in a wider area than before and in a deeper way than before. If you discover clues to unsolved aspects of the mysterious along the way that we have not stumbled across then so much the better. Life will be the richer for it.

Acknowledgments

This book could not have been written without the enormous assistance given by my wife, Hilary. Not only, therefore, is the work dedicated to her but it is shared with her as well.

Thanks are due in no small way to many people for help, encouragement, inspiration, belief and vision. If mention is not made it does not imply ingratitude but merely abject forgetfulness on my behalf.

In particular, and in no order by any means: Cyril Dawson, Joe Jones, Gerald Henshall, Nick Henshall, John Mountain, Mike Oldham, Maurice Winnell, Frank Parker, Dave Jackson, Charles Pickford, Andrew Collins, John Sales esq., J. A. Sutton, Sandra Burgess, Ken Whittaker, John Conliffe, The Woodies, Derek Hulland, Mr and Mrs Pace, Paul Marriott, Cathryn Walton, The Wise Man.

Contents

Location Map

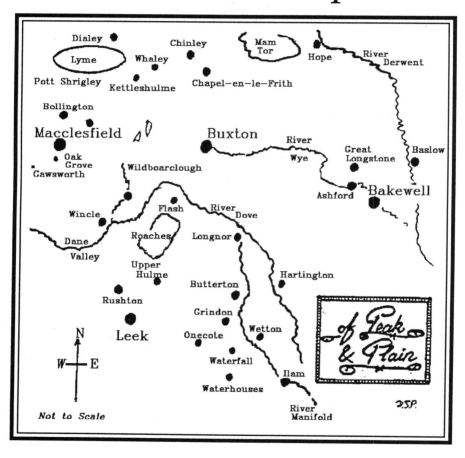

1

VALLEY OF THE GOYT

The Goyt Valley – the vale of the headwaters of the Goyt River – now mainly consists of two reservoirs, the Errwood and the Fernilee, the former being constructed in 1968 and the latter a year before the Second World War, to serve the thirsty population of the southern part of Greater Manchester. The valley has been an agriculture-based area for countless centuries and is criss-crossed by many pack horse trails used to take salt to the east. Later the Catholic Grimshawe family built a stately hall called Errwoood where they entertained on a lavish scale and lived life to the full. A gunpowder factory was there in the fifteenth or sixteenth century and survived until the first half of the twentieth, a span of 500 years or so, only to disappear the same way as Errwood Hall, at the whim of the Water Board. Only ruins of Victorian splendour remain, along with many rhododendron bushes.

The valley is still magnificent, of that there can be little doubt, but it is now a magnificence reflecting man's influence on the landscape and not Mother Nature's alone. Look closely, however, and the magic of the place is still there and although it may be hidden away it can easily be rediscovered.

The source of the River Goyt is on the wild moorland just below the Cat and Fiddle Inn, at the borders of Derbyshire and Cheshire on the Macclesfield to Buxton road. The tiny river, here known as Deep Clough, tumbles down through the heather, bilberry bushes and rocks into the valley before changing its name to The Goyt. It eventually joins the River Mersey near to Stockport but the Goyt Valley is, to most people, that area from the Cat and Fiddle over the grounds of the old Errwood Hall Estate and on to the village of Taxal.

Cat of Seven Tales

The Cat and Fiddle, 1,690 feet above sea level is the second highest inn in England. The popular watering hole was built around 1830 by a Macclesfield banker by the name of John Ryle who was the son of John Ryle a Mayor of Macclesfield (1773) and friend of John Wesley the passionate preacher and founder of Methodism. Mr Ryle junior who built the inn was a silk manufacturer and banker in Macclesfield and in Manchester, the firm being known as Daintry and Ryle, bankers. He was the first Member of Parliament for the Borough of Macclesfield being elected with Mr John Brocklehurst in 1832. He was, like his father, Mayor of Macclesfield (1805).

The internal combustion engine stands alongside a horse drawn coach outside the Cat and Fiddle, a building used as a very welcome stop in the old coaching days: especially during a dark night's journey across the wild moorland. Sir Walter Scott in his book Peveril of the Peak mentioned it as the place where Julian Peveril stopped on his way back from the Isle of Man, at the time of the Popish Plots and Titus Oates.

Mr Ryle erected the Cat and Fiddle on a site that had previously been used for a hunting and shooting box. Regarding the name "Cat and

Fiddle" we have a mystery that has many theories as to the solution. The first is that it is a derivation of *Le Chat Fidele* meaning "the faithful cat" and others are: that it is from Caton Fidele – "faithful Caton", Caton being a valiant Governor of Calais when Calais was in the possession of the English; that the banker got the idea from the nursery rhyme and that it was from Catherine le Fide, wife of Czar Peter the Great. It has also been said to refer to a ball game called "Cat". Mr Ryle was a prominent Freemason and the cat and fiddle features in certain Masonic rites. What had been overlooked in my view is just what was on the site of the Cat and Fiddle before the inn and before the shooting box. Its position high on the hillside and acting as a boundary mark suggests it could very well have been the site of a "Low" or burial ground and the word "Cat" – as we shall see later in the context of Cat Tor – refers to a Celtic site of battle or a burial ground. Perhaps Mr Ryle knew more than we do now. And as to the "fiddle"? Dare I suggest it was a pun used by the banker who later became bankrupt?

Road to the Devil

A Roman Road is said to run through the valley. From Rainow it goes by the hills collectively known as the Great Lows to Saltersford Hall, where it is called The Old Gate, and then up to Pym Chair to the head of the River Goyt proper. Between these two places it is called The Street for about two miles, and near the summit of the hill it is known as Embridge Causeway. Local people used to say this was "made by the devil". From Goyt's Head it stretches to Cracking Stones, here called the Old Road, and then on towards Buxton.

Why should the locals, all farmers, say part of the road was "made by the devil"? The name "Embridge" could well mean "on both sides", meaning the causeway, or ridgeway, on both sides of the ridge of the hill. That seems harmless enough so a little more investigation is needed it would appear. Coming along that causeway to Pym Chair the road turns dramatically to the left, anticlockwise or *widdershins*, which is against or opposite to the "natural" way and therefore un-natural and to the thinking of many, especially in far off times, it must have been made by the devil himself. A possibility, but I think we shall have to probe much further. In Christian times from the ninth century onwards a great deal of what has been termed "earth knowledge" was suppressed. If it did not tally with the teachings of the Church then there was only one description that could be put on it – it was evil, and therefore of the devil.

The stepping stones and farm, at Goyt's Bridge, now submerged in the Errwood Reservoir (Goyt Valley Water Scheme). An old packhorse bridge, it is said it is used by smugglers of salt from Cheshire to evade the Salt Tax. When the Valley was flooded for the reservoir it was reconstructed higher up the valley. The farm building was known as "Apple Pie Farm" because it always had apple pie on the menu at the tea rooms therein, often frequented by the hikers who have so long been apart of the Goyt Valley scene. The sign says "T. B. Broadbent, Goyt Bridge Farm. Teas and Pastry."

This road or causeway led to Pym Chair which is a high or lofty peak and atop this Tor at one time there was undoubtedly either a stone circle, a cairn or a mound wherein the cremated remains of someone, possibly a chieftain or a member of the chieftain's family, were placed in an earthenware pot and buried. These people were pagan (meaning of the earth) and to those early devout followers of Christianity they were of the devil. To their way of thinking, therefore, it was the devil who was responsible for building the road to this pagan spot. But moreso, perhaps the most plausible reason for the association with the devil lies in the word "causeway" itself. It is easily assumed that this refers to a road but in fact it derives from the Anglo Saxon *Cusanweoh*, a seventh century name meaning "The Shrine of Cusa"; *Cusa* being a personal name and presumably of the local head man. The prefix *Em* derives from "hill sanctuary".

Continue westward on the road and the traveller comes to Hernshaw Hill. This name could derive from the heron or hern according to the historian Walter Smith and he may very well be correct in this assumption. Shaw means a small wood. Another possibility, however, is that it could be a reference to Herne the Hunter, the Green Man or Robin Goodfellow of English myth. Perhaps we can note that on the way to the Hill of Herne (or of the heron) is Green Gutter.

Nestling in the valley, but now in ruins was Errwood Hall built in 1830 by a Lancastrian, Samuel Grimshawe. That family lived there until the 1930s when the hall and its contents were sold. This family certainly believed in living life to the full; they entertained lavishly, especially during the shooting season. When not enjoying themselves in the Goyt Valley they would be sailing to all points of the compass around the world. Their estate once boasted 40,000 rhododendron and azalea bushes. The family had a governess, a Spanish lady by the name of Miss Dolores de Bergin, an aristocrat who later became the personal companion to Miss Grimshawe. When she died in her 40s the family built a shrine to her on the moors near to the Roman Road. To this day fresh flowers are placed on her shrine and these flowers keep far longer than any others. Graves of some of the Grimshawes are found on a hilltop above the ruins of the Hall.

Local tradition says there had been a gunpowder factory in the Valley since the 1500s and it is said that powder from there was used against the Spanish Armada. An explosion occurred at the factory in 1909 and three employees died.

The Kaiser's Caterpillars?

Did a German Zeppelin drop millions of caterpillars around the Jenkin Chapel area of Saltersford? An unlikely if not preposterous question you may well say, but some senior Saltersford and Rainow residents are firmly of the opinion that this was very much the case during the First World War.

Since hearing of this strange incident I have spoken to a number of inhabitants of the area who can recall the events that unfolded during the dark days of war in the year 1917, when a plague of millions upon millions of caterpillars descended on the area.

Where the caterpillars came ... around the Greenstacks area. A land of undulating hills and fertile valleys where the story of the caterpillars still lives on.

The Great War was not far from drawing to a thankful close. Most of the men of fighting age were in the battlefields of France unless they were being treated for injuries or had been killed by the Hun. Some remained behind to carry out essential work on the farms. In isolated farming communities, such as the one around Saltersford in the hills above Macclesfield, close by the valley through which flowed the River Goyt, the menfolk were either at war or tending their farms. There were shortages there were hardships and there were many sadnesses. Just like everywhere else.

One youngster who was at the time too young to take the King's Shilling was Les Hill who lived at Greenstacks Farm, just off the road that ascends to Pym Chair (of which more later). This farm became known as Higher House. Les's parents, Mr and Mrs John Hill, were of good hill farm stock and they were a devout Christian couple, tending to the interior and exterior of Jenkin Chapel without any thought of financial reward. Mr Hill was churchwarden and they were both buried in the Chapel graveyard. I hope they found their reward in Heaven. Les passed away a few years ago but he told the tale of the caterpillars throughout his life and recalled the incident very well indeed. A Rainow gentleman spoke to me during the "back end" of 1992, when he was a sprightly 83 about the remarkable events and I must also thank Les's widow, Lizzie, who went to the trouble of contacting his two surviving sisters to confirm the tale.

Here is the story.

The only Zeppelin – a gas-filled balloon powered by propellers – known to have flown over that particular area came one moonlit night in 1917. The exact date has not been ascertained but it was around harvest time. The German aircraft is said to have dropped a bomb at Pott Shrigley but it did not explode and then it turned and flew over the valley, over Rainow and on to Saltersford. It was eventually brought down when it reached the coast. However, that night and the following morning locals discovered literally millions of black and yellow coloured furry caterpillars some one and a half inches in length. They were everywhere. The plague of wriggling creatures appeared to be centred on Greenstacks Farm where all the downstairs rooms were covered inches high with the creatures. Green Booth and Hollowcowhey Farms were also affected very badly. My 83 year old informant told me, "It was though a stone had been thrown in a pool, with the ripples strong in the middle at Greenstacks and they went out for about a mile in circumference. Farms were almost bankrupt after. The caterpillars had eaten everything. There was no grass, no greenery at all growing. There was no food for the cattle and there was no hay to be harvested. Afterwards the area was black where grass and crops should have been."

Little children were sent out into the roads to tread on them, and the farmers and their wives swept the caterpillars out of their homes with brooms or anything they could get their hands on. Some children afterwards helped with shovelling out the bodies as well.

And then the crows came. Apparently "thousands of crows" came from all around and started to eat those furry caterpillars with a vengeance. They gorged themselves until they were so full they could not fly. A lot of them managed to get on to the tops of the drystone walls and stayed there for hours, unable to move off. The walls were turned white with their droppings.

At that time a curate had been sent to the Parish of Rainow to look after the people there because the Vicar, the Reverend Davies, was in France with the troops. The curate's name was the Reverend Edward Vyvyan Kingdom, M.A. who was seconded from St Peter's Church in Macclesfield where the incumbent was the Rev Cholmondley James, a distinguished figure who sported a long flowing white beard. The Curate, a keen naturalist, could not stay at Rainow Vicarage for although the Vicar was in France his family were still in Blighty and so he was billeted to Round Meadow Farm, where the modern housing estate is now. For some reason, perhaps his love of nature, he chose to stay in a tent in the garden.

The Curate and naturalist, the Reverend Edward Vyvyan Kingdom. M. A., who was "seconded" to the Parish of Rainow during the "Great Plague".

As soon as he heard about the news of the plague he set about collecting some of the creatures with the intention of letting them eventually transmute into butterflies or perhaps moths. They were scooped into boxes and stayed with him in his tent.

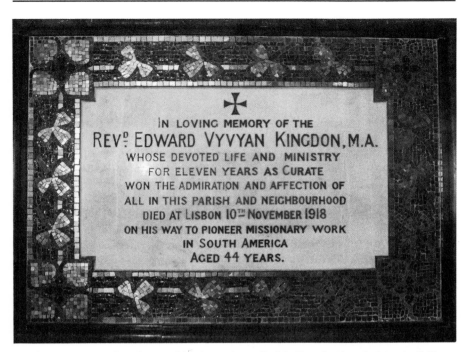

The commemorative plaque which is on the wall of St Peter's Church, Macclesfield.

War finished, and as soon as Armistice was declared the Curate set about making preparations to say goodbye to Rainow and to his church at Macclesfield, for he had intended to Spread the Word as a Missionary before the outbreak of hostilities but was prevented from doing so. Months later he sailed from Liverpool, his destination being the Upper Reaches of the Amazon but he never reached the other side of the ocean. On the tenth day of November 1918, he died at Lisbon, Portugal "of the fever". A plaque at St Peter's church in Macclesfield commemorates his devoted life and his eleven years as Curate. To my knowledge he left no record of his studies into the Saltersford caterpillars.

Many Rainow and Saltersford residents of today recall having been told of this remarkable event by either their parents or grandparents. Very few are actually alive now who witnessed it but thankfully there were, when I set upon the search for the caterpillars, a few. I have been fortunate enough to speak to most of them first hand and what is immediately apparent is that when they say there were millions and millions of the creatures, they really do mean it. It is not an exaggeration. And it was a frightening experience for them, not least because they appeared from nowhere ... dropped from the sky, perhaps, as a secret weapon by an enemy hell bent on destruction? Or was it one of nature's aberrations?

A mystery perhaps never to be solved ... just like many more in that bleak but beautiful area that gets its name from the Salters, the packhorsemen, the Jaggers who criss-crossed Cheshire Staffordshire and Derbyshire before the turnpike roads made life so different. These rugged and earthy folk have left their marks all over the area we are exploring in this book. We have already come across references to them and there will be many more. The centre of this area could be said to be Jenkin Chapel – at least it is the spiritual centre. Where the chapel in the valley now stands there was a preaching cross at the crossroads. It stood there until about the turn of the twentieth century in fact, in the middle of the two roads that cross outside the church. No-one preached from it at that time: it was used only by local children to play on and around.

One of these packmen or drovers was called Jenkin and it is believed he held gatherings at this site. Later, in 1733, locals built the church. Another theory to its name, however, is that when voluntary contributions were being sought for the construction of the church the person who held the bag into which the money was placed would say "It's Jinkin" every time coins were deposited.

Puzzle of Pym

Let us, for a while, explore the Saltersford Valley and see what riches there are for the treasure seekers. Moving left from Jenkin Chapel (a site, I am sure, of gatherings extending back to pre-Christian times countless centuries before Mr Jenkins began to preach at the cross there) the traveller goes towards Saltersford Hall. A walk of about five minutes brings us to this old house which bears the date and initials above its doorway "I.H.F.1593". An outbuilding has the initials and date "R.T.1755". The initials on the house are a mystery but the outbuilding ones must refer to a Turner, descendants of whom are still living in both Rainow and Bollington. The hall is now a farmhouse but at one time it was the country house of the Stopfords, a corruption of the name Stockport, who had their town house in Macclesfield called Bate Hall, now a pub called The Bate Hall, or more commonly "The Bate". There is a story that Cromwell's troops besieged the hall in Saltersford which then had a moat around it and it held out for days. The late Mr Walter Smith, a historian of note who wrote *Over the Hills*, once said that he was shown a large pewter dish that had been hidden with other valuables in a haystack during that period and were not discovered. But there is an anomaly here because James Stopford fought with the Parliamentary Army in the Civil War, and for his military services he received a grant of lands in Ireland and was created the first Earl of Courtown. It is said that Oliver Cromwell once stayed at the Bate Hall as a guest of James Stopford. Perhaps it was the Royalists who besieged the Hall?

This connection with the Roundheads and Cavaliers could tie in with the strangely named "Pym Chair" which stands right on the top of the ridge by the roadside at an altitude of 1,547 feet which has, among other things, an association with the Civil War. Or rather it once stood at this site for there is nothing left of the landmark now, save for its name which is now given to the region atop the hill. To get there walk or drive up Pym Chair Lane from Jenkin Chapel and there is now a conveniently marked car park. Pym Chair was a large stone in the rude form of a chair. At the turn of the twentieth century bits of it were still here but cracked into two parts. Two letters were cut into the stone, one in each part, about five inches high – PC for "Pym Chair". Now its has gone. Perhaps it was broken for repairing the road as some people believe or perhaps it was smashed up because of its associations with something sinister. Let us investigate.

We have already visited the site of Jenkin Chapel where a religious person preached at a mark stone on the crossroads before the church was erected. Some half a mile or so further on, at the site known as Pym Chair, it is thought by some that a similar thing happened. This also was a site for a religious gathering in an isolated spot away from the eyes of the authorities tradition says, and the preacher was someone called Pym. But what religion was it that had to be conducted in secret? There have been several that have suffered from persecution in the past and it may have been any one of these. It may also have been a religion that reared its head before Christianity as we shall see in a little while.

Another answer to the question "Who was Pym?" is that he was John Pym, the gentleman commoner who zealously fought for the Cromwellian cause. It is said that he and his troops crossed the ridge and he sat down on the stone shaped like a chair at that time. This could, indeed, fit in with what did or did not happen át Saltersford Hall only a short distance away. If the hall was being besieged by Royalists then perhaps the Parliamentarians did come to the rescue although it is extremely unlikely that Pym himself was leading them.

Bleak and beautiful. The peak of Pym Chair looking over to Taxal.

So what other strange tales are told of Pym Chair? Mr Walter Smith once received a letter from Miss Gaskell, daughter of the Gaskells of Ingersley Hall, Bollington. Her family was related to the Grimshawe family of Errwood Hall, the stately home now in ruins thanks to the Water Board's flooding of the nearby Goyt Valley for a reservoir. Miss Gaskell told him that there was a band of highwaymen who located themselves on the old Roman Road on the hill now called Pym's Chair after their leader, Pym, who caused the stone chair to be erected to watch more comfortably the packs of mules laden with merchandise proceeding along the roads visible from that summit and who used to send his men down to waylay and plunder them. Miss Gaskell added that the chair was intact until 1838 when her uncle was away in the south of France with his invalid mother and on this return, to his great annoyance, being a keen archaeologist, found that it had been broken up to mend the road, She concluded: "My mother and he constantly passed this chair as they attended Saltersford Church, called Jenkin Chapel." Miss Gaskell's letter refers to the landmark as "Pym's" Chair, the only reference I can find to it being written with an apostrophe. The first edition of the one inch Ordnance Survey map, published in the early 1800s, refers to its as Pym Chair.

However, the most likely solution was unearthed late in the nineteenth century by Dr J. D. Sainter in his *Scientific Rambles Around Macclesfield*. This learned scholar wrote: "The title has arisen from there having being depicted the natural resemblance of a chair in a part of the rocks, with the back, arms and seat fairly represented. It is now all but obliterated. Probably from the Celtic word *pim*, *pin* or *pen*, a height or lofty position." Thanks, doc.

Grove of the Thunder God

Two places for the gathering of worshippers within a stone's throw of each other must mean that the area is significant in some way or another. Add a third and the pieces of the jigsaw begin to fit into place.

For this we must put the microscope onto an area called "Thursbach" one of the last outposts of the Saltersford which is a descent of five hundred feet or so into the valley below. The stream in the valley is Todd Brook that raises a mile further up under Shining Tor, a peak associated with the Otherworld that we shall be investigating. Thursbatch was the site of a solitary and secluded farmstead around the time of the Great War and before in a *hope* or cul-de-sac valley. It has the Tors to the east, Andrew's Edge and Wild Moor on the west and the ground that rises to the Buxton road on the south. The north opens out to Saltersford. Thursbach is the name given to the area around where the farmstead stood. It is a traditional name deriving from *bach* meaning a stream and *Thurs* denoting Thor or Thunor, a god venerated by the early inhabitants of our isles. Thunor, god of thunder, was the farmer's friend worshipped by the Anglo Saxons and also by the Jutes. He was a weather god, the deity to be called upon for the right conditions for good crops and the one to be sacrificed to.

These early Britons had temples to the god, wooden framed simple structures in forest clearings possibly by a sacred grove or a tree of great importance. Religious ceremonies followed the changing patterns of the year and the "priests" who conducted the ceremonies were head men of the districts, their descendants to later become initiates in other religions. Thursbatch was one of the chosen places where the god Thunor or Thor was worshipped in this valley beneath the towering Tors, at the altar by the stream.

These "Tors" display some of the boldest and wildest moorland scenery in this part of Cheshire, the highest point near Shining Tor being 1,837 feet above sea level which is not equalled in either Derbyshire or Staffordshire. On walking southwards along The Tors from the Old Gate (part of the Roman Road) Cat's Tor is arrived at. This is quite simply, some rocks jutting out near the edge of a precipice some 90 feet in height. The word *cat* or *cath* is Celtic again and means either a place of battle or the site of graves, sometimes marked by monoliths. There is little doubt according to Dr Sainter, and I am inclined to agree, that these circumstances denote the locality of a fierce struggle. Nestling at the foot of Cats's Tor is Thursbach.

Peak of Visions

So what, now, of Shining Tor? The loftiest peak in the area, some 1,833 feet above sea level, Shining Tor is not in fact the highest peak in Cheshire as many believe. That distinction belongs to Black Hill on the Cheshire and Yorkshire border, standing at 1,908 feet.

How did Shining Tor become so named? It has been said the reason is because it catches the first rays of the morning sun but then so do all the other hills around. The hill itself is of an even, conical, shape with a gentle rise but the ground is rather rough. Black rocks crop out at the summit and from the top there is a magnificent view of the Cheshire and Derbyshire hills. In Old English, a cliff or hill visited by a "spectre" meaning an apparition or a vision is, according to Brian Branston's fascinating book *Lost Gods of England*, called *Scinna*. Shincliffe (or Shining Cliff) in County Durham derives from the rootname *scinna* and means the cliff of the spectre – exactly the same as Shining Tor (or hill, or cliff) of the Spectre. So just what spectre visited Shining Tor, or just what vision in fact was seen up on those lofty heights? I would ask you to bear in mind the visions or apparitions that are witnessed by devout and holy people of many religions throughout the world and over the centuries. Time and time again the Virgin Mary appears to believers as does Buddha or Mohammed to followers of those faiths. To followers of the religion of the earth, oft times called "pagan", a vision of Herne or perhaps a vision of the Mother Goddess may materialise. We know that just below Shining Tor the Thunder God, Thor, was worshipped at one time because the name is still retained in the geography of the area, and therefore it is not outside the realms of possibility that Thor the Thunderer manifested himself into the minds and therefore the vision of the ancients at the spot.

Wizards and Witches

Whenever, over the centuries, there was a combination of isolated rural areas and, therefore, closely knit communities reliant on the seasons for their living then fear of the unknown was almost bound to rear its head. The area in and around the Goyt Valley was no exception to this and Saltersford, Rainow and Kettleshulme abounded with tales of witchcraft and wizardry. Of course the strong sense of puritanism which pervaded the area did a lot to instil the fact into people's midst that this "religion" (for that is what is was, and still is) was evil. It is during these times that the "evil" women and men who practised the "arts" were said to steal young babies and, if imaginations were extremely rife, they were also said to eat them. They flew on their broomsticks and they cursed the cattle and the crops for whatever reasons took their fancies. Or so it was claimed.

If there was a natural disaster like the hurricane or tornado which wreaked havoc across the Macclesfield Forest and Goyt Valley in July 1662 then someone or something had to be blamed for it. The church could not put this blame on anything holy, so, therefore, it was something unholy. That meant something un-Christian or anti-Christian and the prime suspect or culprit had to be the "old" religion of earth worship. Therefore, anyone still practising this or rumoured still to be practising it was the scapegoat. A witch, in fact, although what in fact often happened was that a person (often called a Wisewoman or

Wiseman) would be called a witch and punished. More often than not this Wisewoman or Man was merely the village herbalist or unqualified doctor, a midwife perhaps; someone who knew how to tend for the sick and to keep everything in balance. Of course there could very well have been an unscrupulous person who kept the area under their thumb by professing to bring evil on those who did not do as they commanded. A far cry from the people attuned to Mother Nature who used their knowledge (passed down through families) for the benefit of their neighbours (and perhaps a few pieces of silver or copper as well).

This belief in the supernatural lasted into the eighteenth century and, in isolated pockets, carried on until the twentieth century. Indeed, it still clings today and I have heard of a Wise Woman still practising in the Hollinsclough area, just south of Buxton. With the Dawn of the New Age of Aquarius there are more and more people trying to revitalise these (almost) lost practises and people are learning once more the natural ways of healing and the natural ways of living.

It is recorded that in the middle of the eighteenth century there were two witches practising in Rainow and they were undertaking "wicked and devilish acts." Here I am indebted to a fine book entitled *Seventeenth Century Rainow, the story of a Cheshire hill village* by Jane Laughton. Proceeds of this well researched work were going to the Church Centre Building Fund and it is well worth reading. The book refers to these two witches, belief in magic, and a seventeenth century wizard. One of these ladies was named Anne and she was the wife of James Osboston. She was said to have caused the deaths of John Stevenson, Barbara Pott and two others. The second woman accused of the black arts was Ellen Beech, the wife of a collier called John. She was said to "exercise and practice the invocation and conjuration of evil and wicked spirits and consulted and covenanted with, entertayned, implyed, fedd and rewarded them; and exercised on Elizabeth Cooper of Rainow, whereby she languished, and in 8 days died." It would appear that their "victims" were richer people than they but unfortunately there are no more whys and wherefors of the circumstances of the allegations. It is also recorded that, in 1662, a claim was made that Kettleshulme had both a witch and a wizard and this accusation was made by several folk who could neither read nor write. The accusation was subsequently withdrawn, it would appear, but this highlights the fact that it was acceptable to accuse people of being witches, wizards or whatever and no doubt these accusations were more often than not made by people with an axe or two to grind against those they accused.

Derbyshire has many documented cases of people being accused of witchcraft. What is interesting about these is the fact in most of the cases (I would say over eighty per cent) they took place at or near ancient sites housing tumulus, barrows or earthworks. Whenever a tradition of fairy folk appearing has been related in the past then more often than not the same statistic comes to light – the incident is said to have happened at or near an ancient site.

Curiouser and Curiouser

Before we leave the Valley of the Goyt we must travel just a little way down the road, along one of the Salt Trails if that is so wished, to the village of Pott Shrigley, a quaint place of habitation that lies just north of Bollington and Macclesfield. It has a lovely fifteenth century church, founded by Geoffrey Downes. As the worshippers look towards the altar, there on the right hand side they can see the grinning features of the Cheshire Cat, immortalised by Charles Ludwidge Dodgson, also known as Lewis Carroll. The face of the Pott Shrigley cat is exactly the same as the cat depicted in the original drawings for Alice in Wonderland. The obvious question arising from this is just what has Pott Shrigley to do with Alice's Adventures? The answer to this riddle must probably be a quotation from the book itself, just three words: "Curiouser and Curiouser."

First of all, why is there a carving of the grinning cat at Pott Shrigley? The origins of the Cheshire Cat are mysterious and it would be safe to say there is no hard and fast conclusion. There was never an actual animal known as The Cheshire Cat and, as the animal has no pedigree we must assume it is a mongrel (or can that apply only to a canine?) Until Dodgson wrote of "the Cheshire Cat" there was no documentation of the name. The image of the creature with a huge grin from ear to ear is thought to have connection with a cut throat or a garrotted neck. A garrotte is a cord placed around the neck and a piece of wood placed between the neck and the cord and twisted so the cord tightens. It was used as a form of ritual execution and is thought to have been utilised in the ritual slaying of the Celtic man whose body was found on Lindow Moss, some seven miles from Pott Shrigley. The preserved body (thanks

Pott Shrigley Church, home of the Cheshire Cat's face.

to the peat it was in) was discovered in August of 1984 and was given the name "Pete Marsh" or Lindow Man. Subsequent expert examination shows he was a sacrificial victim, most probably to the god Balder or Baal.

The ancient hunting forests of Cheshire, including the Delamere and Macclesfield Forests, were policed by families who had the Crown's permission to kill any felon found poaching from the domain of the royal lands. The usual method employed was hanging and the body left as a deterrent to others – a death similar to the garrotte and a death that leaves a similar mark on the victim – a smile below the face, stretching from ear to ear. Another means of death for the guilty party was cutting the throat. Again the "Cheshire Smile" remained – from ear to ear. The lands of Pott Shrigley were part of the Forest of Macclesfield and next to the church is Pott Hall, the seat of the family which assumed the local name of Pott from the township. The family coat of arms is a wildcat collared and chained; not exactly a grinning Cheshire cat but a feline nevertheless.

So what, then, of the creator of Alice and her Wonderland Adventures? Charles Ludwidge Dodgson was born on 27th January 1832, the third child of eleven of Charles Dodgson, curate in perpetuity of Daresbury Parish, near to Warrington in Cheshire. In 1843 his father was made Rector of Croft in Yorkshire and so the family moved to there. Eight years later, the man to become Lewis Carroll entered Christ Church, Oxford, where he stayed until he dies in 1898. There is only a very fine strand of evidence to connect Carroll with Pott Shrigley and this minute threat is a sentence in a book about him by Jean Gattegno entitled *Fragments of a Looking Glass* which said that virtually nothing is known of Carroll's childhood but his family had connections in Yorkshire and Cheshire. Carroll also took a great interest in the occult and the unusual, as was most clearly shown in his literary masterpiece. He was a member of the "Physical Society".

So there is a small possibility – and possibility is all that it can be until we find something documented – that at some time he paid a visit to Pott Shrigley and its church where he saw the striking carving of a grinning cat. This could have been as a young man when his father was a Cheshire curate or it could have been something to do with the "Cheshire connection" in his family but it can only be surmised.

But there is one more strand to the threads of curiosity. To the east of the main doorway of Pott Shrigley Church there is a carved head, a

The face of the Cheshire Cat, grinning from ear to ear, on the wall inside Pott Shrigley Church.

grotesque to give it its correct title. The stonework is much blackened by the rigours of time and the weather but it clearly has identical features to those of the Queen of Hearts in the Wonderland tale, complete with the familiar ringlets and the "piggy" nose.

The cat figures greatly in local legend although origins of the creature's "pedigree" are quite obscure, just like the Cat and Fiddle name at the inn towards Buxton. I felt the need to look further into the background, into the birthline and ancestry, of this grinning feline. This gave me an excellent excuse, I must admit, for an excursion into the heart of the Cheshire Plain, to the salt pans of Nantwich in fact, where there was and, most probably, still is, a hostelry called the Cheshire Cat. However, this was not the reason for finding and needing the excuse to travel across the flatlands. It gave me the opportunity of chatting to a larger than life character by the name of Derek Hulland who has a superb Alladin's Cave of a shop dealing in old and rare books on Welsh Row. A mine of information on anything Cestrian from pre-history to today I knew that he, if anyone, could get to the roots of the Cat's origins. The only problem I knew I would encounter, if problem it should be, was that I would find extreme difficulty in dragging myself away from his mounds of glorious books and also from his own conversation. And so it proved to be.

But such a pleasant problem is no problem at all and this gentleman, whose own roots are firmly embedded in Cheshire, gave me the lowdown on the grinning cat. Derek's ancestors were the Brownswords, scholarly people with tangible history, and he has inherited their lucid brains and manners.

He told me that the Cheshire family of Egertons have on their coat of arms a lion. When inns were given names to identify them to travellers as places to either visit or avoid, depending on what the journeyman's background (socially or commercially) was, many Cheshire inns took the

The arms of the Pott family, showing the wild cat. Has this anything to do with the grinning cat in the church?

sign of the Egerton Arms; particularly those on land owned by this ancient family.

Many of the inn signs were painted by itinerant jobbers with more of a talent for making money than painting a lifelike picture and so the heraldic shields used to identify public houses were often not quite akin to the originals. The Egerton lion, not the African lion with a huge main but the Syrian lion with a smaller neck of hair and looking much more like the domesticated feline ended up as a grinning pussy cat – the Cheshire Cat.

There can be no doubt that Charles Ludwig Dodgson saw the grinning animal on Cheshire inn signs. So what, therefore, are we to make of the Pott Shrigley Cheshire Cat?

It was Alice, I believe, who uttered three simple words as she looked at the face of the cat in the Wonderland tree and saw it disappear, leaving just the grin. She said: "Curiouser and Curiouser." That must sum up the quest for the cat of Cheshire. Was it a sinister way of showing the decapitated head or simply a badly painted inn sign, and what is it doing to the side of the high altar at Pott Shrigley church?

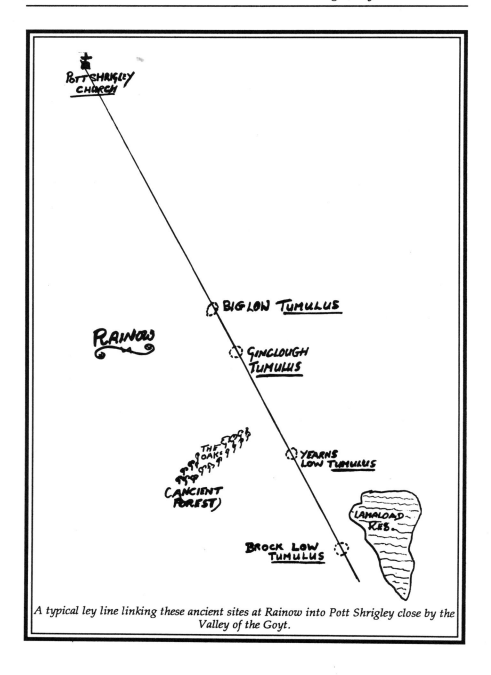

POTT SHRIGLEY
CHURCH

RAINOW

BIGLOW TUMULUS

GINCLOUGH
TUMULUS

THE
OAKS

(ANCIENT
FOREST)

YEARNS
LOW TUMULUS

LAMALOAD
RES.

BROCK LOW
TUMULUS

A typical ley line linking these ancient sites at Rainow into Pott Shrigley close by the
Valley of the Goyt.

2

FOREST AND CLOUGH

Macclesfield Forest and Wildboarclough stand high and mighty above Cheshire, as monarchs looking down from an enormous throne. This majestic land, now indeed a forest as we know a forest today (but once a huge expanse of royal hunting land) encapsulates an area of diverse charms. The conifer forests planted by the Water Board and the reservoirs nestling snugly inside are attractive. The air is richer and fresher up there also; but it is the feeling of the place that is so right. The centuries old farms look like they have become not just part of the landscape but have grown up along with the greenery. They were born of the land not abutted on to it.

And, wherever the walker or motorist travels throughout the area, the mighty pyramid known as Shutlingslow looks down at them. This lofty peak is indeed a pyramid when viewed from most points of the compass and the healing powers attributed to the pyramids of the Egyptians have also been attributed to "Shut" as it is affectionately known. In the years just before the twentieth century, men would rise early on a Sunday morning from the terraced cottages of Macclesfield and walk to the top of Shutlingslow to watch the sun rise.

As historian Walter Smith put it, "What a simple but glorious pleasure! How the blood would quicken in their veins and the spirit rise and thrill within them with every forward step as, pressing over the mountain pastures and past the Oakenclough tarn they beheld in the grey light of morning peak after peak arise; and in the solemn hush of nature newly born they would feel themselves to be in the temple and in the presence of God. But the peak of Shutlingslow with its summit rises before them, and essaying the steep ascent, as length they stand upon its height. Like the Psalmist they have gone from strength to strength ..." What old Walter was saying was that to be on Shutlingslow is an uplifting experience.

An airlift to Shutlingslow in June, 1992. A helicopter was used to carry stone to the lofty peak to construct a public footpath, because the feet of so many trudging towards it were eroding the landscape. According to a correspondent of the Macclesfield Times in 1940 by the name of John Flint of the Crag, Wildboarclough, there had been the sites of two crosses on the summit and also one at the bottom of Oven Lane. Oven was presumed to refer to the King's bakehouse but surely this was too isolated a spot for such a building? More likely Oven refers to the tumulus, shaped like an oven, in that area. Climb to the summit from the very steep side, from the Clough, and there are pillars of stone lying along the way. These may have been on the peak at some time and have been rolled down.

The biblical writer who said "I will lift up mine eyes unto the hills, from whence cometh my help" could have been writing about "Shut" as far as I'm concerned. I have been fortunate enough to experience what those people many years ago have experienced. One winter's morn, cold wet and slightly dark, I and two others trod our weary ways to the summit. In spite of the weather, we stayed there for a few hours and came down from the peak of the natural pyramid with renewed strength and a spiritual upliftment. It had come from within the mountain or had been given to us because of the mountain.

Walter said of Shutlingslow that its peak is like the pinnacle of a temple and likened it to a huge tumulus. He was, in fact, describing the peak exactly how our forefathers of long ago would have seen it. Majestic, mystical and menacing. A place to be venerated and a place to erect a holy shrine upon, just as they did where a line of energy – a ley line – goes across its peak on the way to a tumulus near Rainow (see my book *Myths and Legends of East Cheshire and the Moorlands*.)

Shutlingslow (now for some reason referred to as Shutlingsloe by the Ordnance Survey mapmakers but, in my opinion, quite erroneously) has been inspirational in many ways over the years. It has even been featured in a poem written for Good Queen Bess. This work, entitled *A Golden Mirrour*, was penned by Richard Robinson of Alton in Staffordshire who was a servant in the household of the Earl of Shewsbury, George Talbot. Talbot was one of Mary Queen of Scots' jailers while she was forced to stay at Sheffield Castle.

Richard Robinson was not only a servant but a poet as well, one of those minor Elizabethan poets whose works form such a pleasing background to the mighty literary monuments of the period, not least William Shakespeare's. His third work was *A Golden Mirrour* published in 1589. He dreams, in his work, about Queen Elizabeth, Lord Derby (whose family still possess much of the area of Wilboarclough and the Forest) and the Earl of Shewsbury. Lord Derby is allegorised as "The Eagle", Shewsbury as "The Noble Hound" and the Queen as "The Lyon". The lion Symbol is from the arms of England, the "hound" from the talbot hounds and the eagle from the family crest of an eagle preying on an infant (Eagle and Child Cottage at Gradbach, once a public house, has this symbol over its doorway to this day.)

In the very first verse there is reference to Macclesfield Forest and Shutlingslow, although Macclesfield is printed "Marfield":

"When as the Stately Stagge doth haunt the mountain toppe
And secretlye doeth doubt, the Hunters subtill fleight:
To Marfield Forest, with weary steppes I got.
And Shutlings loe, did scale of monstrous height:
Where faminge brynish flous in th' occident I see,
And sixe sundry Shyres appeared unto me.

These "sixe sundry Shyres" he sees from the summit of Shutlingslow are, rather they were in his day: Cheshire, Derbyshire, Staffordshire, Shropshire, Lancashire and Flintshire. The "fominge brynish flounds" are the waters of the estuaries of the Dee and the Mersey. He goes on to relate how he fell asleep on the peak and was awoken by a loud noise and he went to visit a "Gentle Squire Mayster Leigh of Ridge". Master Leigh was born 1556 and died 1600. The old Ridge Hall where he lived has been replaced by a farmhouse called Ridge Hall. In a stone at the front of the building is the date 1580. As the Squire succeeded his father in 1578 the date on the stone was cut when John Leigh had been the owner of the Hall for two years and perhaps the poet gazed upon the carved date.

Shutlingslow could well be described as the centrepoint of the Forest and Clough – the Forest where only the highborn could roam and where their favourites held the power of life and death over the lowly peasants. After William the Conqueror had set the example by making the New Forest in the South of England, the Earl of Chester set apart the hill country of East Cheshire as a forest for the preservation of deer and game for the purpose of the chase, to find amusement and pastime for the Norman knights and highborn.

In the vestibule of Prestbury Parish Church there are fragments of grave slabs dating from the twelfth and thirteenth centuries and on one of the these is an inscription in which the letters "VIVYN D" are clearly seen but nothing further can be read as the stone is cut off there. It is thought these letters form part of the name Vivian Davenport; the broken tombstone dating back to 1240. The Davenports, now of Capesthorne Hall but originally of Davenport near Congleton and Holmes Chapel, held high office in the Forest of Macclesfield. The office of Serjeant of the Hundred of Macclesfield was give to Vivian de Davenporte by the Earl of Chester about the time of Henry III. The office of Grand Forester of the Forest of Macclesfield was given to Richard de Davenporte by the Earl of Chester about the year 1166. The grant to Vivian was made against his will, in compensation for land his leige lord had "deprived him of". Both these offices were held by their descendants; the Head Forestership remaining in their possession as long as the Earldom of Chester was vested in the Crown. After that, Stewards were appointed until the reign of Edward IV when the office of Master Forester together with the Stewardship of the Hundred and the Forest were granted to Thomas, Lord Stanley.

The Davenports had the power of life and death over anyone they caught in the Forest. If the King's deer was taken, the felon was either hanged or beheaded. A felon's head, dangling from a rope, is part of the Davenport coat of arms to this day and some say was a possible origin of the Cheshire Cat, grinning from ear to ear (its throat cut). This theory is discussed in more detail in the section of this book referring to. Lewis Carroll and Pott Shrigley (see pages 19 and 20).

From the archives of the Davenport family we learn that there was a large number of master robbers beheaded in the time of Vivian Davenport, Roger de Davenport and Thomas de Davenport, along with their companions. The fee for the beheading of master robber was two

shillings and one salmon and for his companions one shilling each. The Davenport's grizzly crest of the thief's head cut short was more than just a badge of office. When they rode through the Peak hills and the Forests of Macclesfield and Leek and the ancient Forest of Lyme dividing Cheshire with the rest of the country it showed they held the authority of killing with impunity – licensed to kill, as James Bond centuries later. In the years from 1458 to 1459, in the reign of Henry VI over 120 persons are named in one writ to be arrested as outlaws by the Davenports.

Numerous gangs infested those wild regions and it appears that the Forest of Mac-

Arms of the Davenports with the felon's head

clesfield was the resort of predatory bands of numerical strength, well organised and led by persons of note. As I have mentioned in another book *Portrait of Macclesfield*, Will Scarlett, one of Robin Hood's outlawed companions is said to have come from "Maxfelt town" meaning Macclesfield. No doubt his skill with the longbow and the hunting of the King's deer in the Forest of Macclesfield stood him in good stead. And no doubt the legends of Robin Hood have grown up around these bands of outlaws and have been coupled with the myths and legends of Robin Goodfellow, the Green Man and Puck, the Hobman of the mists of time.

The present day Macclesfield Forest is an area of England soaked in history, romance and legend. It was the royal forest where the Norman and Plantagenet kings and their successors hunted the wild boar and the deer and hawked for the smaller game. Polecats and wolves roamed in this land also and, no doubt, they were the prey of the royal sportsmen as well. Although the name "forest" implies an area of woodland it was not the case here, as we have already seen. Yes, there were certainly areas of woodland within it but in the main it was wild and craggy moorland and the occasional meadow.

Prominent within the area we know today as Macclesfield Forest is the most beautiful upland vale of Wildboarclough. Today it is the haunt more of the hiker or motorist than of the wild beast and perhaps a smile may be raised by a description of the area in the middle of the nineteenth century by a Cheshire historian called Ormerod. "Wildboarclough" he said "is a district totally uninteresting, a series of moors stretching between Shutlingslowe and the middle of Derbyshire, one of the roads through which is partly the bed of a stream almost inaccessible to any but the natives in the midst of summer." When he wrote that, the roads in that part were used a great deal by wagons and sleighs on which were borne the trunks of trees cut down on the hills and brought down to a charcoal burning station in the Clough.

The Clough is an area known to many and is, as I have mentioned, a prominent part of the present Forest but "Wildboarclough" is the name of a township comprising some 5,000 acres of mountain, woods, streams and meadows that are a continual delight to the resident and visitor alike. Today the names Forest and Clough are synonymous and are, for all intents and purposes, one in the same area but the original Manor and Forest of Macclesfield was on a much grander scale.

The Court Rolls of the Manor and Forest in July 1619, describes the boundaries as follows:

"They say that the circuit of the said Forest of Macclesfield begins at a certain bridge now called Otterspoole Bridge and formerly called Rohehoundesbrigg, and so ascending the water of the Mersey as far as the water of the Guyte as far as certain mosses (or moors) lying between the water of Guyte and the water of Dane Mosse. And so across these mosses as far as Dane-head and thence descending the water of Dane as far as Crumwell and from Crumwell as far as Bramall-hill and from Bramall-hill as far as Rode Greene and thence (along) the Churchgate as far as the village of Gawsworth, the whole of which is in the forest except the Hall and the Church. And so from Gawsworth by the highway as far as the village of Prestbury and from Prestbury by the high way as far as a certain hill, formerly called Norbury Low, lying beyond a house called Bullock Smithy and on the western side of the said road, and from Norbury Low by the high way beyond the house of Robert Handford, leaving that house within the said Forest, as far as the rivulet of Bosdon to the corner of a certain meadow called Barlie Meadow, and thence to a certain little bridge called a Platt, and anciently called Saltersbridgge, and lying within the said meadow called Barlie Meadow and a certain meadow called Riddish Meadow, and from the litlle bridge aforesaid by the high way as far as the said bridge called Otterspoole".

Otterspoole Bridge was near Marple Hall and Crumwell or Crombwell is in North Rode township as also is Bramall Hill, not to be confused with the Bramall near Stockport of today.

All over this area wild deer roamed for no other reason than to be sport for the royal hunters and to be meat for their tables whenever they visited the area. Just prior to the Civil War it is recorded that about 200 head were kept there for the use of the King but this had diminished greatly from the days of the Edwards. Subsequent to the Restoration these forest lands were granted away and enclosed and the Forest as such ceased to exist. Prior to the granting away of the entire forest a "swainmote" court was held at Macclesfield for the Forest and each year all court officials were elected. Offenders against the forest laws were consistently brought to this court and offenders were committed to the gaol to Macclesfield to serve their sentence or to be taken there to be hanged. One place for these hangings was Standingstone on the Ridge near to the Forest Chapel (Myths and Legends of East Cheshire and the Moorlands).

From the description of the boundaries we see the Forest (Latin *forestis* a free space of hunting ground) stretched from Stockport to the Staffordshire border, where it adjoined another hunting forest. This in turn adjoined another and another, stretching all the way to the east coast of England.

Wild Boar or Wild Water?

The magnificent upland vale of Wildboarclough is, each year, visited by countless thousands. They come from all over the world but in the main it is the motorist and his or her family who calls in on the 'Clough for the hour or so of rest and relaxation they seek. Then again there is the hiker who traverses hill and dale to take in the delights of this magical place.

Why do I say "magical"? Well, I was once told by a person who would probably have, many years ago, answered to the description of being a "Wise Man" that the area now known as the Clough was once a place where a healer or herbalist (oft-times called "The Green Man") grew or gathered most of his herbs, plants and roots to concoct his potions. How did he know this, you may ask. I must admit the thought did cross my mind when he told me this and so I asked that very question. His answer was obvious. He still collected this vegetation to make healing remedies as his father, grandfather, great grandfather et al had done. Further, he had always been told the water of the Clough Stream was rather special but only at a very certain time and that time, he said, was "after the Wild Bore had run".

I naturally assumed he had said "Wild Boar" meaning the wild tusked pig that was once hunted in the area and which, it was said, gave its name to the area – Wildboarclough. But what he said about "after the wild bore (or boar?) had run" needed a little more explanation. He told me that the "bore" was a phenomenon peculiar to that area where once in a while (it could be ten years or it could be a century) when certain weather conditions prevailed then a torrent of water or a wave of water akin to a tidal wave – a bore – flooded down the valley or clough. Afterwards, when everything was back to normal the water was believed by some to be rather special, presumably because of whatever it had washed down in its wake.

The water flowing peacefully through the Clough.

There were, when he told me the tale in 1987, two problems as far as I was concerned. The first was that he had not experienced this phenomenon himself and the second was that I was unable to find anyone else who had. So much for the magical water of the wild bore, thought I.

However, on the afternoon of 24th May 1989, memories of what I had been told of the Wild Bore were to be rekindled in a dramatic manner. A cloudburst hit Shining Tor where two brooks rise. The ground was very dry after a month long spell and instead of soaking into the earth the torrents ran into the causeways and turned the brook into an eight foot high wall of water rushing down the normally tranquil valley. The ferocity of that afternoon will go down in history and it took well over eighteen months for the scars of the freak flood which devastated the Wildboarclough and Kettleshulme valleys to finally begin to heal. This eight feet high wall of water rose to a terrifying twenty five feet as it rushed into the Clough. A motorist sadly lost his life as he became trapped in the Bore. Hundreds of sheep and cattle were wiped out and ill-fated cottages suffered thousands of pounds worth of damage as the wall of water crashed down on the picturesque village of Wildboarclough. Traffic and communication were thrown into confusion as bridges collapsed, roads were uprooted and telephone poles and lines floored. Every villager afterwards had their own horror story to tell. The landlady of the Crag Inn said, "I have never seen anything like it." Damage was later estimated to be well over the million pounds.

It was while the hardy folk of the Clough were engaged in clearing up afterwards that a startling fact emerged. There were people still around who remembered EXACTLY the same thing happening in 1932 when a torrent flashed through destroying bridges, washing away walls and carrying cattle miles along the valley. And, some thought, there were people about in the thirties who knew of it having happened before. So perhaps the herbalist who had heard of the Wild Bore washing down all manner of goodies, presumably minerals to be used for healing purposes, had been right after all.

Did this, therefore, mean that the Clough of the Wild Boar was, in point of fact, the Clough of the Wild Bore? I decided to do a spot of investigation and turned to the worthy writers of old and the immediate point to emerge was that Wildboarclough had been known as Wild *bore* clough for most of its existence. The appendage "boar" only came into usage a couple of hundred years ago and before it was most certainly, in all documentation of the area, Wildboreclough. However, in Middle

After the Wild Bore had been unleashed ... the road by Lower Chambers Farm, Wildboarclough, was wrecked and a hole some six feet in depth was made, so strong was the rush of water.

English "boar" (meaning the pig) can be spelt "bore". Back to square one.

So why should the area have been known as the clough of the wild boar? Certainly there would have been wild boar there at one time but just as certainly there would have been wild cat, wild deer and, for that matter wild bunny rabbits and suchlike. So why give it the name "boar"? To have done so would most definitely imply that the boar was there in great numbers but, whilst acknowledging there was most certainly boar there, there is nothing whatsoever in the entire annals of the Royal Hunting Forest to suggest that there was anything unusual about the actual numbers of boars around there. And, let's face it, the unenclosed land would have made it difficult to have confined them to that spot for they could have strayed into the adjoining Forest of Leek or the adjoining Forest of Lyme. There are, most definitely, modern-day references in the vicinity to pigs and boars (but, equally, to other animals as well). Blue Boar Farm in the Forest, which was once an inn, suggests the beast. However, in 1611 the name was written "Blew Bore" and this could very well refer to Blew or Blue after the mossland of a dark livid colour thereabouts and "Bore" meaning a ridge, therefore Blue Ridge. Close by is Wimberry Moss, wimberry being another name for bilberries. There is a Blue Hills Farm on The Roaches, so called because of the blue bilberries that abound there. Just below Shutlingslowe there is Piggford Moor. "Pig" denotes, literally, a young sow or boar but why should these wild beast have needed a ford? Might it be that "Piggford" is a corruption of Pickford, which in turn derives from *Peakford* – the ford by the peak, namely Shutlingslow? Certainly a number of early writers think this is the case, including my old friend Walter Smith for after all there have been as many Pickfords as fleas on a pig's back in that area over the centuries.

So whither the wild boar? It is said that the last really wild specimen in Staffordshire, just a mile or so away, died in 1683 and in Scotland, Ireland and Wales it probably lingered a little longer but the extermination of the species was not due to the hunter but rather to domestication. The wild boar became the domesticated pig. Nearby Swanscoe, near Rainow, is obviously a corruption from "swine" but here we are probably dealing with the domesticated pig and not the wild variety. There's another little spanner to be thrown into the works, I'm afraid, because, adjoining Whetstone Ridge (which reaches 1795 feet, the highest altitude in Wildboarclough) there is Low Bore Edge and in this context, the word "Bore" – as I mentioned in the context of the former Blue Boar Inn – signifies a hill or ridge of land.

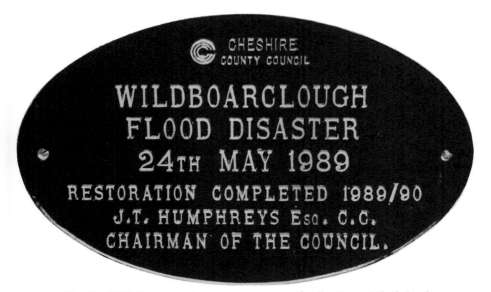

After the Wild Bore ... a plaque commemorates the disaster and the help given afterwards.

So there we have it. Was the picturesque spot in the valley named because it was the haunt of the wild pig? Was it so called because of *Bore* meaning a hill or ridge of land or was it named after the natural phenomenon that returns time and time again to bring devastation to the place?

The Wild Boar public house (highly recommended) would perhaps stand witness to it being the area of the wild boar and so would the Boars Legh, another excellent eating establishment over at Bosley. But the Wild Boar owes its name to a tradition that has only been around a relatively short while and the Boars Legh was the Bosley Chef in the 1970s. In fact the nearest wild animal to meet its doom around the Boars Legh (apart from the incessant parade of rabbits and hedgehogs being squashed on the main road) was a wallaby that a startled motorist knocked down one moonlit night in 1978. It was one of the few surviving wallabies whose predecessors had escaped the private zoo on the Roaches during the Second World War and had strayed with fatal results.

So perhaps it was not the case that the area was named after the wild boar. At nearby Alderley Edge, for instance, names such as The Wizard Inn appeared after a story about Merlin and King Arthur's knights had become popular in the nineteenth and early twentieth centuries and names such as the Wild Boar Inn in the domain of Macclesfield Forest may, perhaps, have surfaced in the self-same manner.

Mercury's Hill

A Force Eight wind was howling and the coldness of the autumn afternoon cut into the openings of our protective clothing as amateur archaeologist Maurice Winnell and I trudged to the top of the peak in Macclesfield Forest known as Toot Hill. This is the tor described as being the site of a Roman encampment, an enclosure for game and a look-out place. The exposed hill and the howling wind on that particular day in early October did little or nothing to support the theory that this was an enclosure for animals and, therefore, a shelter for them as well. If this was early October, what could the bleak midwinter throw at Toot Hill's top?

Many people have put forward many theories about this earthwork on high and perhaps it will take a mammoth excavation before the answer is found; heaven forbid disturbing such an ancient spot just for the sake of curiosity being satisfied. Dr J. D. Sainter in his nineteenth century work *Scientific Rambles Around Macclesfield* said the earthworks on the summit were a Roman camp, although this is extremely doubtful. Whatever they were, at least the dimensions can be agreed upon. The shape is an unequal parallelogram measuring from the bottom of each trench about 190 feet in length from north to south and 150 from east to west. The ramparts of earth could have been three feet high and the surrounding trench the same depth with a breadth of six feet across both at the top. The flat enclosure has two openings, one north and one south.

So why did Sainter and others say this structure on top of Toot Hill was Roman? Well, in those times anything of antiquity was, to their minds, either Roman or Druid. Dr Sainter said the Toot Hill enclosure was "a fair example of a Roman *castellum* or camp" and the Macclesfield Scientific Society were equally certain it was "the famed site of an ancient Roman camp". It was likewise a Roman camp (a station between Buxton and Manchester it was thought) in *Roman Cheshire* published in 1886 and in 1903 the Lancashire and Cheshire Antiquarian Society was calling it Roman. In the early years of the twentieth century there was much activity high on that bleak hill above Forest Chapel, and in 1909 most of the centre was dug to a short distance below the turf, and it was found that on the ground there were flat stones quarried from local stone and of the type used for roofing tiles. About sixty that were unearthed had holes in them and measured some 22 inches by 30 inches and were about two and a half inches thick. Bits of charcoal were also found by the diggers, a few small nails (whether rusted or decayed we know not), some bits of glassware and a piece of baked clay. In 1940 another dig concluded it was Bronze Age similar to other "common types" found in the Pennines, presumably counting the fort on Mam Tor, the Shivering Mountain, among these common types. Then, in 1960, another excavation found indications that there had been a building within the enclosure and concluded it was typical of medieval park and forest sites "probably connected with the Macclesfield Forest".

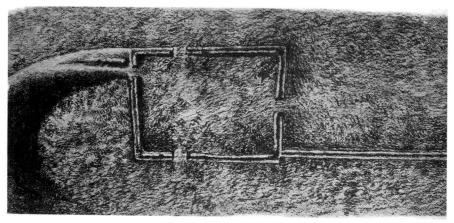

Toot Hill depicted in Victorian times by Dr Sainter.

Interestingly, the late Gordon Rowley, in his work *Macclesfield in Prehistory* refers to a Dr Foote Gower writing in 1774: "About 30 years ago one of these implements of flint, which usually go by the name of

British axes, was discovered within the vestiges of a Roman camp in Macclesfield Forest ..."

So what are we to conclude from all that? The earthworks were first thought to be Roman and built to protect roads nearby; roof tiles and the possible foundations of a building were found inside and an axe, presumably Neolithic, were once discovered there. Oh, and it may have been something to do with the hunting forest. So there it is, but apart from those few bits and pieces, is there anything else? There certainly is, for the name of the hill itself provides a clue. There are a number of Toot Hills throughout Britain. As Alfred Watkins said in the book *The Old Straight Track* a number of writers have connected the Egyptian god Thoth with the innumerable Tot or Toot Hills in Britain, many of which he referred to as "artificial hills." The link seems to be, he wrote, that in the first place the gods Thoth, Hermes and Mercury have a common attribute as being guides over pathways; that Caesar speaking of the gods under the Druids says that Mercury, whom they regard as the guide of their journeys and marches, and to have great influence over the mercantile transactions, is their chief divinity. A Celtic god, Tout, or in its Romanized form Toutates, is supposed to be what Caesar referred to and this name has been found on a Romano-British altar. It is a fact that sighting mounds (he was referring to ley lines) called *Tot, Toot, Tout, Tute* and *Twt* abound all over the Kingdom, and the root is probably Celtic for on the Welsh borders natives call such a mound *Twt* and pronounce it Toot.

This was in the early twentieth century and, returning to our old friend Sainter, the learned doctor wrote in 1878: "*Toot, teut, tew* or *tyr* are Gothic terms for the god Mercury, who was a messenger of the gods and presided over the safety of the highways."

It is easy to assume that the name for the earthworks atop the hill and the name for the hill itself are one and the same. Some writers have fallen into this trap, noticeably the ones who say the earthworks were a pen or pound for game in the Royal Forest and they would be let out to be chased into the Coombes below. The toot, it has been said, referred to the sound of the hunting horn. Why go to all the trouble of digging a ditch? Why not just erect fences if this was the case, why have only two entrances and exits ... surely such things as prevailing winds, the direction of sunlight and other considerations would have changed the directions the animals were released. And why were these gates or entrances aligned with the compass points?

Mercury (or Toot) was also Hermes, the Greek fertility god, who was accredited with good or bad harvests and he is the one to whom animals were sacrificed, especially in the form of a ritualisation sacrifice performed by the Druids. Hermes, Thoth or Theutates was also, as in Mercury, the god of roads. To the Celts, so very strong around this area of Macclesfield until the Romans drove them to the Isle of Mona (Anglesey), he was also the god of war, their chief among gods.

Whatever the reason for this enigmatic earthworks, it is certain that the hill on which they were built – whether as a temple to the god Mercury or as a defensive fortress – was something rather special. A short distance above the encampment in an area known as Dirty Gate, in a field to the left, there is a tumulus now hidden in pine trees which is twelve yards in circumference and two yards in height.

Plagues and Hangings

In the chapter on Fools Nook, the Grove of the Druids, I mention that one of the ley lines or earth lines that traverse the area is coupled with the Plague Stone at Greenway, close to the Hanging Gate public house. Greenway was a road whereon farm produce and animals were moved to the markets at Congleton and Macclesfield. This stone, some five feet or so in height, was definitely not erected as a "plague stone" but was merely utilised as one in the 1600s. Its original use was a thousand or more years before the Plague and then it was an "acupuncture" stone, tapping in to the strong earth current; or it marked a path of the current which flowed on to a spot now known as Three Shires Head, where there were three similar stones marking the conclusion of the "pathway". These became boundary markers when more land was possessed by the monarchy and were, sadly, removed in the nineteenth century; for what reason we know not.

The stone on the Greenway in the ancient Forest of Macclesfield had a cross carved into it either at the time of the plague in 1603 or much earlier when similar pagan stones were being Christianised. Dr Frank Renaud, M. D., wrote in 1876: "Macclesfield was visited by the plague in 1603 and 1646 and on each of these occasions Greenway Cross was used as a plague cross" (We should perhaps note here that it was called Greenway Cross, a definite pointer to it being erected for another purpose). He went on: "to which country people came to sell their provisions to the dwellers in the town. The practice was for sellers to place their goods near the cross and then retire, after which the townspeople came and paid the price marked, letting the money fall into a basin or socket filled with water, by which process all infections were supposed to be destroyed". An honest lot were those townsfolk then, if they put down the asking price when no-one was about. Perhaps there was a cleric there, a holy man – possibly a hermit or anchorite (not uncommon then) – to see the transactions took place honestly. Dr Renaud also referred to a basin being placed there, or a "socket filled with water". There is certainly not a socket to be seen on the stone and it is far too tall a stone for the top of it to have been used, so presumably there was a basin, and it must also be presumed that the "water" alluded to was holy water. It is possible that it may have been urine, though, for that was used as a disinfectant.

By the middle of the nineteenth century the stone had sunk half its length into the ground and had declined from upright until it lay almost on the ground. Youngsters in those days were accustomed to run up it and jump off the end. However, the task of re-erecting it was ultimately undertaken by the parish and was raised again to "something like its original height". This information was recorded by Mr James Beard Thornley, formerly of Wildboarclough, who in the 1930s had gone to live in Nottingham. He wrote about that time: "Its lofty position on the lofty Greenway Hill suggests that it may, for one reason, have been placed there as a guide and landmark in the trackless forest and, bearing as it does, the simple symbol of the cross, may also have been intended by those primitive people who placed it there to be the centre to which they gathered for worship or prayer centuries before any church was built among those wild hills. It certainly was made use of during the plague. My ancestors were residents in Wildboarclough and Wincle at the time of the plague and were, therefore, eye witnesses of the doings around the old Greenway Cross. From that distant time to the present it has been handed down through our family parents to their children that the sellers and buyers met at the cross, and all money which changed hands had to be passed through a bowl of water for disinfecting purposes".

There is also the possibility that the stone marks the burial place of a guardian of the forest or the highway, perhaps a chieftain, perhaps a shaman or holy man. It was certainly at one point used as a wayside preaching place, as Mr Thornley has suggested.

The "Plague Stone" on Greenway, Higher Sutton. Notice the Christianisation of the stone with the carving of the cross.

To the left of the Greenway is a steep slope, Cophurstedge, meaning the edge of the hilltop wood and below is Cophurst Farm. It was at this old house, it has been said, the Raphael Holinshead was born. He wrote *A History of England* and dedicated it to William Cecil, Lord Burghley, who was a minister to Queen Elizabeth the First. William Shakespeare undoubtedly used much of this work for reference and inspiration for some of his plays. Next to Cophurst is Pott Lords farms, strange name indeed, which presumably refers to the Pott family who gave their name to Pott Shrigley. At the bottom of Greenway is another farm with an odd sounding name, Old Dollards. Walter Smith suggested in *Over the Hills* that this name referred to *dal* meaning a division or boundary that could tie in with the stone at Greenway being a boundary stone. I would suggest, however, that it is from *dail* or *dael* meaning clockwise – the only way to walk around sanctified places and objects – in this case our Greenway Stone.

Just over from Old Dollards is a famous hill country inn, the Hanging Gate, which was first recorded in the year 1668, but no one knows how

One of the best known characters in Forest and Clough in the entire twentieth century was this man, Tom Steel.

old it really is. It has a small claim to fame as being the fourth highest pub in the country at 1100 feet. I first came across this hostelry many years ago when its sausages grilled over charcoal behind the bar were famous throughout three counties. Its beer was, then, straight from the barrel and it was affectionately known as "Tom Steel's" even through the landlord by that name had long since departed. Tom was quite a character and he had the misfortune of only having one arm. In October of 1900 when Tom was aged 23 and living at Daisy Bank Farm, Higher Sutton, he was sitting on a wall in a field on the farm with a loaded gun between his knees resting his hands on top of the muzzle and his foot touched the hammer. His right hand was shattered. He was landlord at The Gate for 50 years until February of 1952 when he went into hospital and never came out. He had brought the pub from a Mr Hadfield (of the famous Macclesfield family of chemists, drysalters and druggists) only a few years before he was taken ill, having rented it up until then. He paid the princely sum of £1,400 and a further £250 for two fields. He died in December of 1952 aged 77, some eighteen months after he had electricity installed at the premises (it came to the Cat and Fiddle in April 1955 incidentally) and one of the "regulars" Miss Jean Miller took over the premises, buying the pub and the two fields for £2,600. Tom's dog, Nell, went with the deal. I was once told the tale of someone who took a very "posh" friend to Tom Steel's. This was done purely to see the reaction of that friend when Tom prepared a sandwich for them. Sure enough the instigator of the trip was not disappointed when Tom sliced an inch and a half of bread from a crusty, if somewhat stale, loaf and then cut a wedge of cheese followed by another doorstep of bread. The sandwich was placed, or rather thrown, onto a plate that had to be dusted (by means of Tom blowing on it) and then handed over the visitors. "Do you want any tomato with that?" Tom asked. "No" said the friend. "It's a good job" said Tom, "cos I haven't got any".

Jean Miller, who took over the Hanging Gate from Tom Steel in the 1950s. With her, at the door of the Hanging Gate, is the dog that she inherited from Tom, and called Nell. Sitting on the barrel is one of Nell's puppies.

The stories about Tom are legion. Mr Cyril Dawson of Langley, a lover of the countryside all his life and someone who has spent countless hours rambling and hiking the area told me he used to call in at Tom Steel's for a cup of tea and a sandwich. In the days before the second world war a pub could open at any time for a traveller, providing they had walked over three miles, although Cyril did not partake of alcohol. "I don't think Tom ever took his clothes off" Cyril laughed. "His waistcoat was always filthy, full of grease and goodness knows what else." Once Cyril called and asked: "Can I have a mineral water, Mr Steel?" Tom replied, with his usual stammer: "they con, if it inner frozzen." Tom's brother, Jim, lived at the nearby farm and had the habit of bathing (unlike Tom, it is thought) in a rainwater tub in the farmyard. Many was the time passers by, especially young ladies, has to avert their gaze. Tom was helped out by another local resident, Seth Brunt, who farmed Old Dollards. Cyril told me of one of Tom's pet dogs that used to sleep in the oven for warmth until Tom forgetfully shut the oven door one night and that was the end of the poor animal.

The hanging Gate has a sign:

This gate hangs here
And trouble none:
Refresh and pay and travel on.

An innocent enough sign today but it is thought the origin of the "hanging gate" is a trifle sinister. "Gate" did not refer to a gate as in the farmyard or garden sense but as a path or way from the Scandinavian *gata* and this gate was the entrance or way to a spot where felons were hanged, presumably poachers of the Royal Forest. The pub is recorded in the seventeenth century as "The Gate". For the exact spot of these "hangings" we must perhaps, once again, look to the Greenway Stone's environs some 1254 feet above sea level.

By the Seven Lowes

The environs of the Forest and Clough had, and still have, much to explore. Cluelow Cross and the Bullstrang or Bull Stones have been chronicled in my previous book as have the three crosses removed from various parts of the Forest and now in situ at West Park, Macclesfield.

Bullstrang, the stone circle across the way from Cluelow Cross is most probably a corruption of Baal's Stan or Stone and we delve into the origins of Baal's Stones in detail in the section of this book devoted to the High Rocks, the Roaches.

What is interesting about the area wherein the Bullstrang is set is that it is within extremely close proximity of seven other ancient burial sites – in fact, in the self same field. In the Survey of the Manor and Forest of Macclesfield, 1611, there is a section that reads: "Item one parcell of ground called the Seaven Lowes lying west and being of the middle sort containing 135 acres". Sainter shows seven circles on a plan. Today, they are no more, presumably under the plough or dispersed in some other way for some other reason than agriculture. In 1819 the seven lowes were recorded and one of them was said to have been opened and proved to be a large cairn, fully fifty tons of loose stone having been piled up, with a slightly baked or sun-dried British urn containing ashes in the centre.

Northwards from Seven Lowes we come to an area known as Nesset and here there was, on Bryant's Map of Cheshire for 1831, a spot marked "Burying Field". Walter Smith in a newspaper article in the 1930s entitled *Forest and Clough* thought this was from *byrgen* meaning grave, thus a grave in a field. Just north of Nesset and near the foot of Teggsnose (now a country park based at a disused quarry) there is evidence of an ancient burial. In the 1870s labourers who were working at a reservoir at the vase of Teggsnose hit a sepulchral urn with a pick-axe, some three feet down.

Cinerary urn with flint arrow head, found at Langley

It contained burnt human bones of a young person and a finely polished flint arrowhead. The urn was eight inches high, seven and a half wide and tapered to four inches at the bottom. It must be presumed that back through the mists of time there would have been a stone of some description on this grave. Near the head of the reservoir at Langley there is a large conical mound looking like a tumulus, and a little further in towards the Leather's Smithy pub, near to a farmhouse on the left, there is another tumulus. This farmhouse is called High Low and this apparent contradiction in terms is easily explained. Low means, as we have already seen, "Burial mound", thus the high burial mound.

An old photograph of a famous hostelry in the Forest of Macclesfield, Leather's Smithy, named after a family who once carried on the trade of blacksmiths at the site.

Here we let Walter Smith wax lyrical for a while. He wrote in the 1930s: "From these memorials and remains of the dead found on the hills we can safely say that these hills were peopled by a tribe of family of a rude and simple civilisation nigh two thousand years ago. And from the hill name Shutlinsglow we may deduce the tribal or family name Scyttelingas, or as we now say, Shutlings."

UNVEILING CEREMONY

OF

MEMORIAL STONE

TO

ℳr. 𝔚alter Smith

AT

Standing Stone, Macclesfield Forest,

Saturday, 12th May, 1951

At the area of Macclesfield Forest known as Standing Stone there is a memorial to Councillor Walter Smith, the person who wrote Over the Hills and also a series of newspaper articles called Forest and Clough. This area on the crossroads above Forest Chapel was a place where suicides were once buried and where hangings of forest felons took place, but the beauty of the area makes it an outstanding spot for a memorial to a fine man who knew and loved the area so well.

By the way of a slight diversion here, perhaps I can relate the tale of a brown trout at High Low Farm. This particular fish warranted a photograph and an "obituary" in the Macclesfield Courier of 13th October 1949, when it passed away at the remarkable age of twenty years. The paper recorded that the fish had lived in a cattle trough at the farm for twenty years. Mr H. Slack, who occupied the farm, said the fish had been caught by his nephew, Geoffrey Shrigley, when the fish was only about eight inches, in a stream which runs at the back of the farm. It was put in the trough along with other fish, all of which died or disappeared. This fish was nearly eighteen inches long when it died.

Way back in the nineteenth century, long before the days of mechanised fire engines, there were strange happenings at a farm fire that occurred in the district. Late one Saturday night both the Macclesfield Corporation Brigade and the old Volunteer Brigade were called to a hayloft fire at Wettonway Farm and both engines, drawn by horses, went to the scene. It was, apparently, always a race to see which brigade could arrive first and on this occasion the Corporation men were first on the scene. There was an unwritten agreement that the officer in charge of the brigade arriving first should take control, but in the case there appears to have been some sort of difference of opinion and orders given were not complied with. A reporter of the day wrote: "A still more regrettable state of things has been recorded. The water had not been poured on the burning building more than five or ten minutes when much to the astonishment of the officers of both brigades the supply suddenly ceased and it was found the men responsible for the pumping had gone into the farmhouse to be refreshed and were subsequently found enjoying bread and cheese. All the while the men lower down the road were pumping and, of course, as the water pumped by them into the well of the engine farther up the roads was not pumped from the latter through the hose and on to the fire, it overflowed and was running to waste along the road".

"The dispute between the brigades was the subject of much shouting from the spectators who took sides. Meanwhile the fire burned briskly and the members of the household were at their wits' ends, throwing furniture, bedding, etc., out of the windows, while the crowd noisily clamoured round the door demanding refreshments, which were drunk indiscriminately, so much so that no less than three 18 gallon barrels of harvest beer were consumed as well as everything there was eatable in the house".

"Hosepipes were turned on the crowd to get them away. After about half an hour's delay, water was again directed on the burning building, the flames were got under control and the building saved." One can well imagine what a stir all these happenings created among the quiet living people of Higher Sutton.

These quiet living people had not a church to call their own for centuries until the Church at Sutton, dedicated to St James, was built at a cost of £2,000 and opened for divine service in 1840. There was no church in the immediate area and the building was erected "because of an accumulation of evil in the area." Representations were made to the church authorities and part of the official "petition" said of the "accumulation of evil" that "Invited by the natural beauty of this portion of Sutton, and by its apparent unprotected condition, the thoughtless youth, the wild and dissolute of both sexes from the town of Macclesfield had converted it into a kind of Sunday playground, and on that day the once peaceful hills were made to echo to the loud reckless shout and shriek of vice and folly."

3

GROVE OF THE ANCIENTS

A grove, once sacred to the Ancients, is still very much in evidence today. Its name is Fools Nook.

As the motorist careers along the A523 trunk road between Macclesfield and Leek and, hopefully, notices a road sign warning "slow down" and restricting speed to 30 mph, the driver is entering this Sacred Grove of the Ancients. There is little doubt very few will be aware of just what is and has been there; perhaps those graced with the perception of the third eye and, of course, those with learning of the past will perceive immediately where they are; although then again I am sure there have been many who have sensed there is something "different" about the place. Side by side with the roaring and racing motor traffic, brightly painted barges or narrow boats chug and glide their peaceful way along the Macclesfield Canal through this self same Grove. Again, few pleasure seekers on that waterway will have an appreciation of the place, most will be enjoying nature's copious beauty and will, perhaps, be noticing their pulse rates have slowed to the pace that is life on canals. A waterhen or hopefully a heron will be more of a distraction than fields that once housed the fairy folk (and some say still do), a grove where the ancient wisemen (oft-times called "The Fools") held court and where our forefathers (and mothers) buried their warrior chieftains.

Fools Nook nestles some two and a half miles outside Macclesfield and its main claims to modern fame are a welcoming hostelry, now called The Fools Nook, and a notorious swing bridge over the canal leading to a twisting stretch of B-Road heading towards Gawsworth, and nicknamed "The Corkscrew". This area, which is still home to a small part of what was an ancient forest is also a melancholy place, a place where sadness has been at times. It is not my intention to dwell on this aspect of the Sacred Grove for too long and so suffice to say that over the years there have been far too many horrendous accidents and fatalities around here – both on the road and on the canal. Just why this should be will perhaps become more apparent as we look around this grove of much mystery.

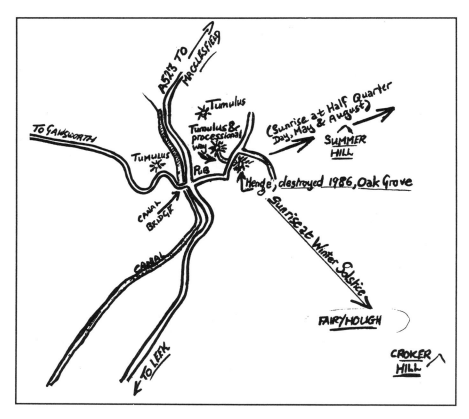

The area around the Nook of Fools.

The area was, and indeed still is, officially termed Oak Grove, an obvious reference to the fact that it was a spot in a forest – the Lyme Forest that for centuries was the boundary of the Earldom of Chester with the rest of the country. This huge forest, stretching from Ashton Under Lyne (or Lyme) in the south down to Audlem (or Audlyme) near the Shropshire border in the south was first chronicled by a Chester monk called Lucius shortly after the Norman Conquest when he wrote that Cheshire "was shut in and separated from the rest of England by the Wood Lime". A journey from north to the south will give us the names "Lyme" at Lyme Park in Disley, Lyme Handley (the seat of the Legh family) neighbouring on Macclesfield Forest which would separate Cheshire and Derbyshire and Staffordshire, Lyme Green in Macclesfield (or Sutton to be correct), then Linley (or Limeley), Newcastle-under-Lyme and Audlem (Aldelime or Old Lime).

The Forest of Lyme, a natural boundary for the Earldom of Cheshire.

Whilst relating to boundary names, Macclesfield could well be the Mark in Field, meaning a boundary mark or *merk*, or *meer*. In the ancient Lyme Forest there are other "lyme" references. Burslem, now part of the Potteries, originally was Bure-wardes-Lyme and Madeley was formerly Madeley-under-Lyme. A Charter of Randle Blundeville, Earl of Chester, dated 1218, after granting certain privileges and laying down services his Barons should perform, declared that because of "great services" they did for him in Cheshire none of them should do him service "beyond the Lyme" unless of their own free will and their own cost. This Forest of Lyme was clearly owned by the Earls of Chester and when they wanted to place an Abbey in the farthest outpost of their domain they chose a wooded vale in the Lyme – just outside Leek (Dieulacres). From this we can see that Leek and also Newcastle, now both under the jurisdiction of Staffordshire, were part of the Cheshire boundary.

But to return to Fools Nook. There are several names around this spot which still stand witness to it being part of this huge forest. Those names refer to the oak tree, the species venerated by Celtic Druids. The inn was formerly called The Royal Oak and the large hall close by "Sutton Oaks". Nearby is Broad Oak Reservoir, not to mention Oak Farm.

What indeed was, and still is, special about Fools Nook is the fact that the Grove has a number of earth energy lines which nowadays, because of quarrying, because of the digging of the canal and because of the construction of the turnpike road have been broken, twisted and dispersed with the consequence that they have changed, unfortunately for the worse. These workings have combined to make a site once powerful with natural energy forces a place which now emanates as a Black Spot.

So why has the area become known as the Nook of Fools? For one thoughtful point of view I should like to refer to a gentleman whose work on local history I admire greatly, the late Mr Walter Smith. In his work entitled *"Over the Hills"* he wrote: "Below Croker Farm and Hawkshead Quarry lies the little hamlet of Fools Nook or Oakgrove as it is now officially known. The only explanation of this name which I have received is that the 'nook' is a corner or bend in the Old Road at Hawskhead Quarry; the 'fool' in this case being the man who planned the road – it was a 'fool's nook'. This explanation does not appeal to me, and I submit the following as a more likely rationale of the name. I have shown some words are formed by *aphesis* (letting go) of some prepositional letters and the coalescing of the remainder with the following noun. Thus 'atten ash' (at the ash tree) has become 'Nash'. If 'atten ash' is spoken quickly there is little heard but 'Nash'. So, also, 'Nalder' for 'atten alder'; 'Nelms' for 'atten elms' etc. Middle English forms of 'oak' were *ook* and *oke* which by the process described became *nook* and *noke* and if this process has taken place at Fools Nook then the name means 'fools at the oak tree or oak wood'. Sevenoaks by a similar corruption has become *Snooks*. We thus see 'oak' in the name and ... the thought suggested is that certain merrymakers (who were the 'fools') met at a certain oak tree ..."

Mr Smith was certainly correct about the corruption of "Nook" from "at the oak" but his merrymakers or fools around the oak tree has gone only part of the way towards a solution. Before we reach that solution let us look at other thoughts on the name "Fools Nook". One suggestion has been made that the area was a favourite haunt of a court jester, Maggoty Johnson who graced the splendid Gawsworth Hall. Samuel "Maggoty" Johnson – so called because his brain was supposedly in such a state it was likened to being eaten by maggots – was one of the last of the paid English jesters. His other nickname was Lord Flame because of a notable character in a play of his that was performed to a degree of success in London. His fame indeed lives on in the shape of Maggoty Wood in the village where his grave lies. Maggoty is said to haunt the village of Gawsworth and his ghost still rides a white horse thereabout. The area of Fools Nook just about lies in the parish of Gawsworth and the pub sign depicts a court jester or fool. But the real reason for its appendage goes back many more centuries, I feel, than Maggoty's time.

Before we journey back across those centuries let us look at two other possibilities for its name both of which have connections with the journey on which we shall shortly embark. The County of Cheshire is rich in tradition of Mummers' plays (still held at Antrobus and Chester as Mystery Plays) and present day Morris dances owe much to their origins. The dances often feature a character known as "The Fool". A custom connected with these plays and dances was the election of a Lord Misrule (or Fool) by men who dug out marl top dressing for farms from the side of the road. These men, known as Marlers, had a "Lord of the Pit" whose function it was to collect money in the summer from passers by and share it out at the end of the day. Whichever person had given the most cash would have it proclaimed by the bunch of marlers that "Mr So and So" had given "part of one hundred pounds".

Preparing the rushes for the annual rushbearing ceremony at Forest Chapel. Mr Bill Bullock (foreground) had been plaiting the rushes for every ceremony over the previous fifty years when this photograph was taken in the 1950s (C. Berrisford).

The second possibility connects with the rush-bearing ceremonies so popular in most village churches up until the twentieth century. Now, only the tiny Chapel in the Forest – St Stephen's in Macclesfield Forest – retains its rushbearing ceremony during the month of August but at one time churches such as Wincle, Prestbury, Gawsworth and Bosley all had this tradition of bedecking the floors, walls and pews with freshly cut rushes. Perhaps a reason why this died out can be appreciated by the following: a "Fool" was often associated with this ceremony in bygone times. The cart that was ceremoniously filled with rushes and taken to the church was accompanied by a Morris and also a Fool, chosen for the occasion. Often this fool was a female and referred to as a Bessy. No doubt the religious establishments cleaned up the merrymaking over the years while others merely called a halt to it. What took place was certainly not what the church of today would condone. Today in Macclesfield Forest the charming ceremony is organised on purely Christian lines and it is a devout spiritual and uplifting service I would recommend to anyone who has not attended. There is no indication of what could have taken place in the past, although in the church accounts for 1848 an item that may be associated with The Fool and merrymakers can be found. It appears that after the service five shillings was paid "To William Smith for Repairing the window at the Chapel and School, broken at the Memorable Rush Bearing". See my book *Myths and Legends of East Cheshire and the Moorlands*.

Let us now examine what is, in the opinion of many, the real reason for the name "Fools Nook" or "Fools at the Oak."

The Christian Church's Feast of Fools (Regis Stultorum) was a Festival that, like so many, was a Christianised form of a pagan ceremony. The Church took the view in 601 AD that where "temples and altars" of pagans were to be found a church should be erected or, if not, the temples should be sprinkled with holy water at the very least. What the Church also did was to make pagan festivals into Christian ones, a prime example being Easter. In the year 1220 a cleric and chronicler named Thomas of Chobham wrote: "It is known that until now there has been the perverse custom in many places where on any holy feast day wanton women and youthful fools gather together and sing wanton and diabolical songs the whole night through in the churchyards and in the church to which they hold their ring dances and practise many other shameful games. All such activity is to be prohibited with the greatest diligence, if it is possible. However, it is encouraged in many places for many men would not otherwise come to such feasts if they could not play games."

The feast of Fools was held over the Christmas season, despite a ban being placed on it in 1236. Apparently on 1st January in most churches there was custom whereby divine service was interrupted by "Fools" and general mayhem reigned throughout the "Feast", the festival or festivity. This ritual was a reversal of roles, when the nobles and ecclesiastical hierarchy were "humbled" by being dressed in rags and tatters and the poor reigned for the duration (although goodness knows what retribution may have been dished out afterwards).

To early Christianity the name "Fool" was placed upon a person who was not Godly, or someone who denied God by making Christians suffer. In the Mystery Plays "The Fool" is more often than not brought to the forefront during the trails and tortures of Christ. In these performances Christmastime, when Christ was born, is a time for rejoicing and this is done by taking part in pagan "Fool Games" wherein morality defeats festivity.

From the fourteenth century Fools became an identity and were professional entertainers at the courts of nobles. They were people of great personality although oft-times physically deformed. They were owned by their masters.

Early Christianity used "Fool" for a person of little or no wit who consequently could not, it was thus thought, appreciate Christianity – usually rustics who, although living with the Christian Church, still followed some, if not all, of the old earth worship rituals. The "Witless Fools" often had impersonators who preferred not to "have their wits about them" for their own sinister reasons. Today a parallel would be the dabblers in Black Arts. As we have seen with the Marlers and the Jesters "Fools" became an entertainment and also an excuse for people to participate in high-jinks. In parts of Cheshire and Derbyshire there was a mock beheading ceremony during the performance of a ritual dance – later associated with Morris dancers and Mummers – which suggests a deeper meaning for there is here a distinct remembrance of the Celtic Cult of the Head which is dramatically symbolised in Gawain and the Green Knight when the Green Knight is beheaded by Gawain at Yuletide. This time of the year, a Christianised festival, was the feasting time around the midwinter solstice, and the time of the Feast of Fools.

What this tells us has, I hope, become clearer. Fools Nook was once the domain of pagans who practised their own religion rather than that of the established church. This Nook or Grove in the Forest was undoubtedly a Sacred Grove of the white-clad Druids as well as the green-robed philosophers known as Ovates and the wearers of the blue robes, the Bards. These Celtic shaman or holy men, the initiated, were said by the Roman chronicler Tacitus: "They (the Druids) had the care of education. They alone cultivate knowledge; they conceal from the vulgar the secret doctrines in which their pupils only are initiated. They determine the litigated questions; it is their business to allot rewards and punishments."

It was documented by Julius Caesar and others that the oak was sacred to the Druids and the mistletoe that sometimes grew on it was known as the all-healer. Taken in drinks it imparted fertility to barren animals and it was believed to be an antidote for every poison. Gaillic (the language of the Celts) gives the name *uilioc* meaning all-healing to mistletoe and the Greek name for the oak tree is *drus*, no doubt the root of the word Druid.

In this mystical area, where the Christians said the "Fools" practised their heathen ways, people who lived before the Druids also found it special. There are at least two tumuli in the area (there were many more but they have gone under the plough) and a processional way linking burial sites. We shall be looking at these in more depth but for the time being let us put ancient man and Druidic rites to one side and explore the world of the fairy folk – a world many believe existed around Fools Nook.

Domain of the Fairy Folk

At the southernmost part of the Nook is an area called Fairyhough. The word "hough" is old English from *hoh* and means the end of a ridge where the ground begins to fall sharply, a bank. The reference to Fairy will bring us back eventually to Druids and pagans but before then let's explore the enchanted world.

Throughout the Three Shires there is still a belief, albeit lurking in the backwaters of the mind, that fairies have not only existed but are here today. These tiny folk are not at the present time seen as winged creatures (fallen angels) but are for all intents and purposes smaller versions of us mere mortals. Belief is far stronger in rural areas and it is here that names such as Fairy Hill, Fairy Field and Pixie Corner (at Rushton Spencer) live on. Or, as in the case of Fools Nook: Fairyhough (there is also a "Fairy Glen" close by to the south). Some farmers in the Peak still leave a bowl of milk outside for them and, if an animal should lap it up then it is unfortunate for the fairy folk will seek revenge upon it. If the farmer doesn't leave milk then a cow will, surely, dry up. A tale is still told of a young girl visiting Leek Market. She saw a small man with a reddish nose and saucer-like eyes stealing juicy apples from a stall and so she shouted to the stallholder. As she did so the tiny man disappeared, presumably into the crowd. This girl set to for a long walk homewards towards the craggy peaks of the Roaches. As she paused for a rest she noticed this tiny person by the roadside. He berated her for telling tales and it was only then that she realised just what he was. Only many years later would she tell anyone outside her close family of what happened next: the little person told her she was to lose the use of limb of her choosing. She did not believe him and mockingly said it had better be her little finger; by the time she got home she could not use it and this lasted throughout the rest of her life. The family (I know them extremely well indeed) instructed everyone to keep quiet about the incident and the girl was unable to perform a task she had done so very well up until that incident – churn butter.

The story was told to me by a member of the family who is, today, an extremely well known Medium.

The tiny clay pipe found over one hundred years ago in a Kettleshulme field with the tobacco still lit. It has been said that it is a "sample" pipe used by salesmen to take around to traders to inspect and then place their orders. However, close examination shows it was undoubtedly a well-used pipe as the tobacco staining is very much in evidence. It is also extremely tiny as comparison with a two pence piece shows. Was it a fairy pipe or was it a sample pipe? I will leave the choice to you.

In the Dane Valley food was left for the fairies in fields the night before they were ploughed. At Kettleshulme a tiny clay pipe with a bowl of less size than a farthing was found in a field. A lad, tradition says, saw the little folk dancing in a circle and ran towards them. When they saw the youngster they fled, leaving the fairy pipe, still with tobacco in it and still smoking. When fungus springs up in fields and woodlands in North Staffordshire they often sprout in ring formation. These are known as fairy rings. In the Manifold Valley, where sunlight is scarce because of the high rocks blocking out the sun's rays fairies are said to light the way for travellers. Perhaps these are will o' the wisp known locally as Jenny Burnt Tail. Of Lud Church chasm in Back Forest near the River

Dane it used to be said the fairies danced at dawn outside the entrance to the Otherworld – a fissure in the rocks going way below ground. Gawsworth, the village that sprouted romance and legend in abundance was once the setting for the annual "Dance of the Good People" or fairy folk around the village cross and a similar event was said to take place at the village cross of Mottram St Andrew.

At Wincle in the nineteenth century if a window was broken and glass was not readily available for repairs, cobwebs were collected to fill in any gaps after the hole was boarded up. This, it was believed, kept out the "Brownies" or hobgoblins (cobwebs were also a useful source of first aid. I have been told of a Swythamley farmer who badly cut himself on the arm and ran into the shippon where he scooped as many cobwebs as he could and placed them on the wound.)

Around the Dane Valley area, food was left in the field the night before it was ploughed "for the fairies". In this evocative picture, Frederick Goodwin leads two fine horses at the plough at Hammerton Farm, Wincle, about the year 1930. Frederick later lived at Parkgate Road, Macclesfield, and served in the Voluntary Fire Service during the Second World War. (This and some other old photos of the area appearing in this book thanks to Dave Jackson of Macclesfield).

Many references to fairies have a pronounced Christian trait, most particularly that they are fallen angels – seduced by Satan. When Michael evicted Satan's hosts from heaven they were followed by countless innocents and when God saw heaven was emptying He raised His hand and closed the gates but some had descended to the earth's mountains and woods. Another Christian reasoning for fairy folk is that Adam and Eve became parents of so many children that they were ashamed. God asked Eve to bring then up them to Him and she hid half of them but God knew and said all those hidden should be "hidden from mankind"; thus they became Huldre or the Hidden people.

Most of the beliefs in fairy culture today centre on Celtic areas such as Ireland and Wales and Scotland but there is still a strong lingering belief in rural areas of England, not least around the area of Fools Nook. The Grove at the Nook of the Fools was undoubtedly a Celtic Special Place and could possibly have associations with the later rural belief that fairies are the dead (or those who have gone before) as others say ghosts are the dead. In this case those who had gone before would have been the pagans or the "Fools".

David MacRitchie in his 1890 book *The Testimony of Tradition* told us that belief in fairies stemmed from the memory of an earlier race of small people, pre-Neolithic cave dwellers or earthwork dwellers who used flint arrowheads and had "Much knowledge of the hidden paths" (ley lines) in their country and were said to have power over the weather and possess other magical skills. He researched into the theory of the existence of "a conquered race" lurking in woods and mounds and hanging around farms doing casual work for food "but distrustful of their conquerors' clothing as a badge of servitude". Might this have referred to the heathens conquered by the Christians?

Folklore looks upon fairies as ancestral ghosts still retaining earthly bodies, being tolerated but venerated and, indeed, pitied for their lifestyles and beliefs – exactly how early Christians looked upon the so-called Fools or pagans at the Nook in the Oak Forest. As Katherine Briggs in her book *The Vanishing People* states: "The distinction between the feared and venerated spirits of ancestors, nature spirits and the remnants of ancient mythology is very hard to draw."

In *Magical and Mystical Sites* Elizabeth Pepper and John Wilcock write: "There are those who feel a connection exists between fairies and Druids. Celtic lore reveals a long-standing belief that fairies are a kind of spiritual being who retain the otherwise extinct teaching of the Druids."

The ancient cross at Mottram St Andrew, pictured about 1905, where the fairies or "good people" were said to dance around every year.

Enigma of the Lights

There is a lot more still to be said about this area of Fools Nook. As a newspaperman I have, in fact, reported on many strange events in the area over some thirty years or so and, no doubt, there will be more to come. One occurrence in that spot over many years has been the repeated sightings of light and bright objects in the sky and other sightings of a curious nature. Many reasons have been given for these close encounters of whatever kind or another over the years, and it is interesting to note that one put forward by a number of researchers is the fact that they often taken place at spots where ley lines are dominant.

The first time I came across reports of sightings of unidentified flying objects around the area was when the G.P.O. mast at Sutton Common, or Croker Hill to give its proper name, was being built in the early 1960s. This huge concrete object with dishes and transmitters sticking out of it like a pin cushion is one of many that form a chain across the British Isles, and the site for its construction, to the east of our Grove and less than a mile away as the crow flies, was chosen no doubt because of its uninterrupted vantage point high atop Croker Hill. What was never taken into consideration was the fact that it was the spot of an ancient burial mound and one of the Beltaine fire sites where ceremonial and sacrificial fires were lit and fireballs were rolled down into the vale below. There is a strong possibility also, although nothing has ever been chronicled, that Croker Hill was a beacon site; one of the lofty tors where beacons were lit to signal danger. Beacon Hill on the Edge at Alderley is definitely such a spot and Mow Cop on the Cheshire and Staffordshire border is one other. In the area around the Grove, another Beltaine fire site was Kerridge Hill where the monument White Nancy now stands.

But to return to the strange sightings. Around the time of the construction of the Post Office tower, four motorists travelling along the Macclesfield to Leek road in the vicinity of Fools Nook saw what they termed flying saucers shoot out of the hillside behind Fools Nook and in front of Croker Hill. These lights or UFOs or whatever hovered around the building site and shot off.

Two weeks later, a car was waiting at Bosley cross roads on its way from Leek towards Macclesfield. One of the passengers in the rear seat saw a silver glowing craft, like a disc, come towards their vehicle and hovered above. The passenger, a woman in her forties, did not say anything. She was shocked, scared and did not believe what she was seeing. The car drove on towards Macclesfield and the object stayed over it. As the car neared Fools Nook the vehicle's lights went out. The driver cursed and drew to a halt and the UFO shot off at a great speed. The lights came on again. It was then that the passenger told the other what she had seen.

But the sightings were not only confined to the Swinging Sixties, when everything that was seen was not always what it appeared to be. In the 1970s I spoke to a man living on the Hurdsfield Estate of lights shooting out of the hill just to the east of Fools Nook. These lights, only a few inches across, were, he said, darting about here there and everywhere and he likened them to Tinkerbell, the fairy in Walt Disney's cartoon version of Peter Pan. The hill he was looking towards when this occurred was at Fairyhough.

And on to the eighties. A party of scouts were walking the Old Leek road in broad daylight during the August of 1985 and the all, some twelve in number, saw a silver and blue cigar-shaped object hovering in the sky and then disappear. In 1989 there were reports of strange objects in the sky above Kerridge Hill where the white folly proudly stands. One Bollington resident followed them in his car and lost sight of them at ... you've guessed it. In 1991 a man waiting for the swing bridge to close on the Macclesfield Canal across from the Fools Nook inn looked into the sky (it was about three in the afternoon) and saw a silvery object travelling much faster than any plane. And so it goes on. As we have seen, ley lines are often given as a reason for these sighting and, with the aid of divining rods, I and a friend, Mike Oldham, tracked a very strong one which goes slap bang through our Grove.

Following the Paths

There is a pastime that I and a number of other people often indulge in. If nothing else it gets us up out and about in the fresh air but, far more than that, it is an ideal way of re-discovering the dragon paths. Let me explain.

Our marvellous Mother Earth has, on the surface of her body, or rather just beneath it, myriad lines of energy. These lines known at the moment as ley lines, were "tapped into" by our forefathers who built megaliths of stone at certain chakra spots upon them. Where a number of these energy lines or paths converge, then it is a safe bet those of whom have gone before were able to find them and utilise their strength. An obvious example is Stonehenge where extremely strong lines emanate although they were stronger before a road was built alongside and concrete laid for a car park. Old churches are often sited on these lines for one very good reason – the sites were places where pagans met and drew off the energy before Christianity used the self-same spots. When the Christians Church defeated this "evil" the storytellers had St Michael or St George defeating the dragon (that which was un-Christian, just like the Fools at the Oak) or in some case the Worm – meaning exactly the same. Notice just how many churches sited on hilltops, the favourite spots for dolmens or stone monoliths, are now dedicated to the dragon slayers, George and Michael. Look at carvings on crosses or other stonework carried out by Christian Saxons and it's a fair bet that somewhere there will be dragon or worm being slain. Prestbury Church has one and so does Leek. There are many others.

The tower at Gawsworth Church with close-ups (see next page) of the serpents, dragons or "worms" leading the seeker to the ley lines. Another line goes from here to Astbury Church.

Close-up view of the 'dragon'

To return to the pastime previously mentioned. The two dragons' path followers tended to be myself and a healer by the name of Mike Oldham who lives in Leek. We usually chose a Sunday morning to find a suitable spot where there was likely to be a strong ley line and then follow it. The way this was done by means of divining rods, two pieces of metal that detect these energy lines in the earth's crust. We had, usually, a fair idea where to start our journey – just find an old church, pick up a strong line with the divining rods and follow it. They tend to be, we found, anything from three miles in length to twenty miles or more. There is one line, I am told, from Stonehenge in Wiltshire that reaches Arbor Low in Derbyshire, although that one has not been travelled by anyone I know. One of the delights of following these dragons' paths is that we do not know where we are being led or what lies along the paths. However, on every occasion the paths have concluded at a pre-Christian site of one type or another.

Our journey along the particular ley line that took us through Fools Nook began at The Edge at Alderley one frosty January morn. We had gone to Castle Rocks on the Edge, with the assumption that there would be a strong line or two from there which may take us across the Cheshire Plain or there again lead us up into Derbyshire, but we were to be disappointed. Certainly there were lines and they had, our divining rods told us, been very strong ones at one point but they were now decidedly weak. We put this down to the quarrying that had taken place for probably two thousand years at and around there (although we were later told the real reason may have been the immense psychic activity that had been undertaken, both good and bad, over the years). So disappointed were we that we agreed to call it a day and began our drive home but, for what reason neither of us can say, we both voiced the opinion that Gawsworth Church would be a good place to visit to see if there were any ley lines from there. And after all, the beautiful setting enhanced by a crisp and clear Sunday morning would be a bonus.

When we arrived a few minutes later, we were not disappointed in our choice. Majestic swans were gliding across the lake, the holly bushes were laden with ripe red berries and the clear blue sky reflected onto the crystal clear water. The backdrop to this delightful picture was Gawsworth Church itself and as we walked through the lychgate towards the ancient building we both sensed we would find something. And find something we indeed did. The first sight to greet us as we approached was a skull and crossbones chiselled into both gateposts surrounding the churchyard. No pirates here and the dead we were most certainly not afraid of, but of what were we being warned by these double carvings? A stroll around the church brought the information, via the divining rods, that there were four extremely strong ley lines, energy lines or dragon lines coming from the site of the church. That in itself was not unusual for, as I have mentioned, most old churches come complete with their own lines and here, at the Church of St James, we did indeed have an old church – there was mention of one on this site in 1265 AD, although the present fabric was built in the fifteenth century.

As Mike was walking forwards, a divining rod in each hand, I happened to look up towards the tower and saw them. Four dragons, one on each corner of the square tower and each one pointing in the direction of a ley line. Paths of the Dragon indeed; if ever proof was needed there it was.

Our time was up for the day, and, as good people were starting to walk towards the church for the Sunday morning service and we did not wish to get in their way, we decided to start our explorations at another time. The first ley line we eventually followed, with the dragon's head pointing our way one hundred or so feet above, took us in the direction of Fools Nook. Just before Fools Nook, the line crosses a Neolithic barrow or burial mound at Woodhouse End. This barrow was excavated in the 1960s by Mr Gordon Rowley, a remarkable man who had "the eye" for spotting these earthworks. He took a University degree in archaeology in later life and became the paramount expert on ancient earthworks in the locality. The vast majority of his many finds can be found in the Grosvenor Museum in Chester.

St George and the Gawsworth Dragon: extract of a mural by J.F.A. Lynch in 1851. This was, it is thought, on the North Wall but it was vandalised in the Reformation and later whitewashed over.

Over the crossroads at the Nook and on the old Leek road we went, and then over the hills and far away to Higher Sutton where the next landmark of significance we came across on our ley line was a stone monolith at the side of a road. The local name for this stone has been, for many years, the Plague Stone and the story has been that this is where people came to during the time of the Plague and left money in vinegar on top of it so as not to pass on the deadly visitation. Goods to be purchased were left at the same stone. It does indeed stand on an ancient trading route named Greenway, a road along which livestock and agricultural produce used to be taken to market but our first reaction on seeing its size, some five feet or so, was that it was one heck of a stretch up to leave the money. Surely something a little smaller would have fitted the bill a little better.

If this stone was erected at the side of the road for the purpose tradition says it was, then it was placed there by Christians, as there is a cross clearly carved into it. However, could it perhaps have been there before Christianity and only later had the "evil" cast out by the

Christian symbol? Some days later, I drove a psychic medium up to the spot and she "saw" the stone in its entirety. At one time a head was on the top and a sword was by its side – a warrior knight standing guard, with a breastplate marked with a cross. We got out of the car to stretch our legs and there, on the grass at the base of the monolith, was a piece of stone in the shape of a sword handle. It fitted perfectly onto the right-hand side of the "knight" exactly where the sword handle, projecting from the scabbard, would have been. The next weekend, Mike and I continued tracking the ley line. It came to an end at Three Shires Heads where the boundaries of Cheshire, Derbyshire and Staffordshire meet.

The pack horse bridge at Three Shire Heads where the line from Gawsworth Church terminates. William Farrar, licensee of the Queens Arms (Macclesfield) and George Hall pose for the camera before the First World War.

The next time we went on a journey of exploration armed with divining rods and great expectation, we let one of the Gawsworth dragons point us in an opposite direction. This ley line took us to Upton Grange at Upton Priory, on to Prestbury and the Norman Chapel in the churchyard and through to Adlington Hall, the home of the Legh family for centuries.

Might I suggest any reader with the will to "dowse" a ley line follow the other two? The dragons on the tower will point the way. It is extremely easy to make two L-shaped pieces of metal from old coat hangers. Perhaps a little practise in the back garden beforehand may by advisable. Just hold one in each hand very loosely, stretch your arms and focus your mind on what you want to dowse – probably drains would be the easiest at first. Then walk along and see how the "rods" react. Good luck.

Processional Way

Before we leave this rather special place, there is something more to investigate. As we have seen, albeit briefly, the Grove is also the site of not one Barrow, but at least three and between two of them there is what could possibly be a Processional Way.

The largest – and the one that has been investigated fully – is the Beaker monument Barrow at Woodhouse End, just over the main road and canal. This tumulus (SJ96/914695) was excavated entirely by volunteers led by the late Mr Gordon Rowley from September in 1966, and lasted almost exactly two years with work taking place at weekends and afternoons and evenings, whenever the demands of earning a living permitted, but was held up from November 1967 to March of 1968 because of an outbreak of foot and mouth disease in the area. All the finds and all the records are safely housed at the Grosvenor Museum at Chester, and the site has been restored to as near as possible its original condition. Large amounts of pottery and flints were found as well as two stone hammers and two pieces of jet rings.

On the other side of the road, behind Sutton Oaks there is a tumulus which has a tree growing from its top and an ancient portway or processional way runs from it to where another tumulus stood for over two thousand years but was removed in the late 1980s because of the demands of modern day agriculture. It is difficult, if not impossible, to discern where this barrow was but thanks to the efforts of the team of searchers led by Gordon Rowley and including David Bethel, Ruth Collier, Pam Huges, Kath Lowe, Matin Pedley and Maurice Winnell, the site was documented before being lost under the plough.

A tree now grows on the tumulus at Oak Grove

The fact that this area contains these number of barrows or earthworks shows that those who came before the Celts venerated the area as much if not more. Perhaps we have touched upon the reasons why so many people throughout the centuries have found the Grove so special but, there again, perhaps there is much more to be found.

From the tumulus at Oak Grove, the remains of a processional way can still be seen. This led to a spot off the old Leek road where an important example of linear earthworks used to be until the 1980s. The late Gordon Rowley described it as being oval, lying roughly on a north-south axis with two apparent entrances. He said it had an inner bank some three or four meters high and he thought it resembled a henge type monument, possibly Neolithic. My thanks to M. Winnell for pointing this processional way out to me.

Top: The year is 1967 and the cremation urn is removed from the Bronze Age barrow at Fools Nook. (Congleton Chronicle). Bottom: the barrel alongside the beaker most probably contained beer or other alcoholic brew, to help the occupant of the burial mound on his journey to the next life. Picture: M. Winnell.

4

VALLEY OF THE DANE

Sacrificial Waters

The Dane rises on Featherbed Moss, a desolate stretch of Axe Edge Moor not a stone's throw from the source of the River Goyt. Tinkers Pit, a remnant of the days of the travelling pedlars and supposed rogues who made counterfeit coins, is close by, at the convergence of the A537 (Macclesfield) and the A54 (Congleton) roads to Buxton. The baby Dane trickles south-westward through Dane Bower Quarries, and quickly grows and gathers pace as it tumbles under the packhorse bridge at legendary Three Shire Heads to Gradbach, running in the fern-clad valley below Midgleygate and being joined by Black Brook by Black Forest, the realm of Lud's Church (the Church of the Celtic god Llud). On, by the side of what is left of an ancient forest it goes, joining with Clough Brook, which occasionally causes havoc in The Clough and then cascading swiftly over rocky outcrops to Danebridge and Wincle, fed here by a stream that runs by the scene of a battleground of long ago, a stone circle and the burial ground of a chieftain. By the shadows of Swythamley, the spiritual resting place of a great Earl of Chester, it runs through Heaton and under the Leek to Macclesfield turnpike at Hug Bridge, the boundary of Cheshire and Staffordshire. In fact the Dane acts as a boundary for most of its course before rolling through Cheshire. It gathers apace across the plains of Cheshire, through Havana Mills and Congleton and then ever westwards.

The river itself was named by the Celtic peoples who were in the area before the Romans came and who returned in smaller numbers when the mighty Legions left. They called it after their Earth Mother, Dana or Danu. The land where the Dane rises and then runs through is littered with remnants of these people, especially in names associated with the sun god Baal, whose followers lit the sacrificial Beltaine fires. There is also this remembrance in the name of a farm at Quarnford, Ann Roach, the rock of the mother goddess, Anu or Danu.

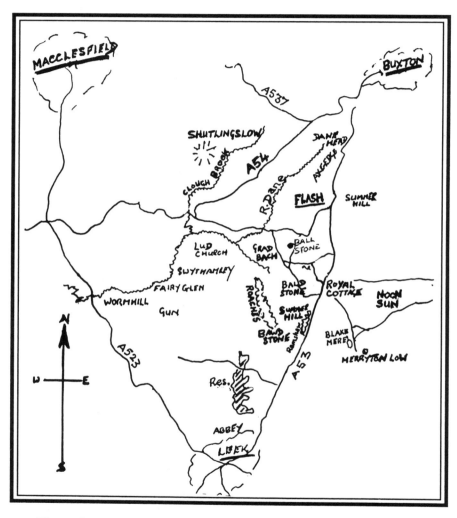

The area between Macclesfield, Buxton and Leek. Most of the places shown are mentioned within this book. Below Swythamley there is a spot that used to be called Fairy Glen, and further along the River Dane there is a relic of the earth power in the farm name, Worm Hill – on a dragon path. See the chapter 'Land of the High Rocks'.

The mother goddess's river was so named out of reverence to the spirits that this race of romantic warriors held for water. Life had to be given, at times, to appease the anger of the spirits of the water and this Celtic deity cult blossomed into Derbyshire where the springs and wells that brought forth the elixir of life, water, were worshipped and thanked. Close by the Dane, at Rushton, a well dressing ceremony was held until the middle of the 1920s. Offerings were made at these fountains, much as we today throw coins into a well or a pool to "make a wish" and then, in those far off times, it was to appease, to thank and to plead for health or wealth. Whether or not the Dane was a river thought possessed by either angry or benign spirits we do not know for certain, but there is something there to give a very strong clue, and it can be almost conclusive that Clough Brook running into the river was possessed of an angry sprite if it is, indeed, the "wild bore" of the Clough.

We can be reasonably certain that in the days of the Celts some sort of sacrifice would have been made to the spirits believed to reside in the waters. It can also be reasonably concluded, for it was the accepted way of worship, that sacrifices would have most certainly been animals and most probably humans.

Where, then, would they have taken place? It is unlikely they would have just occurred anywhere; there would have been a special "holy" place and this site of ritual sacrifice is still there, for anyone to see. At Danebridge the road to Wincle met by an old trail from Swythamley, and also by a well-defined path alongside Hangingstone Farm and the Hanging Stone itself. This huge rock has, on many occasions over the centuries, been described as a sacrificial stone or an altar whereon sacrifices took place. Most areas have a stone with this tradition attached but its "polished" flat top (thought by a good number of people to have been placed there by human means) certainly adds a lot of weight to the tradition. In Victorian times the scholars of the day were, to a man, convinced it was a "Druid" stone although everything ancient to those good doctors and professors was either Druid or Roman. But maybe they were spot on here. There is, without a doubt, a path around the Stone which could very well have been a processional way around it, sunwise, and then on to the Dane where is a natural pool on the river's southern side (the same side as the processional way) that may well have been the place for the sacrificial victim to be thrown in, either already dead or to be "finished off" by drowning. Perhaps a ritual garrotting had taken place as at the black pool of Lindow Moss just a few miles away where the preserved body of Lindow Man was unearthed and shown to be a sacrificial victim.

In a two mile stretch of the River Dane from Gradbach to Danebridge the immediate vicinity contains many legendary and magical points of renown. There is Lud Church, the cavern of the Green Knight, the sacrificial hanging Stone, an outpost of a holy order, Wincle Grange, a well (Honeyfall Well, where the sweet water flows), an ancient cross in the grounds of Swythamley Hall and a tumulus. In addition, the Hall was once a hunting lodge with very strong associations with nearby Ludchurch and the saga of Gawain and the Green Knight. It is where the Norman Earl of Chester chose to have his heart buried – many miles from his seat of power at Chester and even further from his family home across the Channel. Further, a few strides from the River Dane near to Bartomley Farm, there is a stone circle and also an ancient burial ground, where gold objects were discovered and where treasure seekers have mutilated the site for many years in the vain hope of finding anything more.

There is no doubt whatsoever that the river is something special and its valley stands witness to this fact.

A Walk in the Wild Wood

We have already mentioned Back Forest which extends from The Roaches down to the Dane and perhaps this is the time to take a walk into that wild wood. Back Forest, an ancient woodland on steep and craggy slopes tobogganing down to the Dane Valley is a dark and haunting place worthy of a Gothic horror story. Lofty pines compete with tortured elm, red-berried rowan, hearty ash and bedraggled beech. The floor is a carpet of heather, rocks, blackberry creepers, moss, and the gnarled roots of trees. Walk amid its awe-inspiring splendour and you will not see the sky, only the occasional shaft of golden sunlight penetrating the gloom. Its silence is broken by the cry of a bird, the rasping of a fox or (if you listen very carefully) the drone of the river below.

Several well-worn paths trodden by the feet of centuries meander through. Walk them carefully; there are fox and badger holes to trap the carefree; there are exposed tree roots to trip the ungainly, slippery embankments to embarrass the reckless and rocky outlets to tumble the careless. Such is the make-up of a dream. This tree-tangle is the same now as when our forefathers trod the paths on their way to a ritual of worship at the green chapel of Llud. It is the same now as when their forefathers trod the paths.

The casual trekker could walk from one end of the forest to the other end and miss the very core of this place, the heart and the soul. The reason why no-one has axed this stretch of woodland because of the awe it inspires.

Lud Church

This is the crevice named after Llud and it is where legends have been manufactured, as I will now tell.

It was accepted for some time, certainly in the nineteenth century and most of the twentieth that the tale of Walter de Lud Auk and the vanquished Lollards who sang in nature's chapel, hidden from persecution, was the reason for the place's name. There was also a romantic point about the sweet singing of his granddaughter. Those who have my other book may remember I did not think this was a true tale and still am of that opinion. It was all poppycock and I have now heard verbal evidence to support this contention. First of all, Frank Parker, who is mentioned in another section of this book as being a source of great inspiration to me in my quests, set me on the trail of someone employed by Sir Philip Brocklehurst, Lord of the Manor of Swythamley. It was Philip Brocklehurst, Bart., who was the author of a book that brought to light this charming tale of the sweet young thing who was killed, in a very romantic way, because of the sweetness of her voice, etc. This lady whom Frank told me of is from a respected family still on Goldsitch Moss, and she was employed at one time by Sir Philip to take money from visitors to Lud Church, who had been attracted there by the romantic tale of the Lollards and the sweet singing.

A pony and trap brought trippers from Buxton to Lud Church, courtesy of the enterprising Sir Philip, and an entrance fee was charged to witness the scene of the legend written about by the landowner. The lady who took the entrance fee, perhaps one penny, was given a cap and a shoulder bag and I understand that at one time a gate was placed across the entrance to the chasm. At that time there was a figure of a lady clad in white nestling on a crevice in the rocks in the side of Lud

The figurehead of the good ship Swythamley perched in the magical Lud Church before latter-day vandals knocked it to the ground. At that time there were five small caverns but these have been blocked off.

Church. This was in fact the figurehead of a ship named *The Swythamley* because of the financial backing of the Brocklehursts. Sailors called it the Sweet Emily but visitors to Lud Church were led to believe, by the Brocklehursts, that it depicted Alice de Lud Auk, the sweet young thing put to death in the cavernous rocks.

I mentioned this to Maurice Winnell, the amateur archaeologist who has shown me many ancient sites in the area, and he added confirmation to this point because he remembered that as a boy in the thirties he and some friends walked from Macclesfield to Lud Church, and were there met by Sir Philip's gamekeeper who charged them, if memory serves, threepence to enter the cavern.

But what cannot be doubted about the place is that is, and was, something special. The rocks from around the area were looked upon as something rather different, possessing an energy that could be used to advantage; amulets carved from the rocks were sold by enterprising locals and were worn around the necks of people in need of protection, particularly from the Evil Eye – the curse put on crops, livestock and people by the black witches, the evil ones, who professed to hold power over their fellows. Whether any tangible power was utilised is uncertain, but one capability these evil folk did possess was the knack of frightening people into believing they could be harmed.

In 1992 I was in regular contact with one of Britain's foremost researchers and writers of the earth mysteries, Andrew Collins, and one aspect we assisted each other in was the magical Lud Church area. Andrew writes in his extremely interesting book "The Circlemakers" about his theories concerning an energy called orgone, and ties this with the properties contained in rocks in the area and also mud from around Lud Church that was also used to make talismans.

The previous year, Hilary and I and some others visited Lud Church. One member of the party, then a young teenager, psychically tuned in to an elderly woman who made the young lad move his hands, rubbing them together and shaping something that was unseen to the rest of us. Afterwards she said, through him, that she earned silver from this but she had lost some and could we help her to find it. There on the footpath in front of us the teenager spotted and old sixpence, glinting in the afternoon sunshine. It was not until I told Andrew about this that we both realised that, perhaps, the youngster, when shaping something with his hands, may well have been moulding the marl or clay for a talisman.

Much superstition has abounded, and still does for that matter, in and around the Valley of the Dane. Of Three Shire Heads, for instance, the Reverend Beresford said in 1864 that it was believed the reddish yellow ochre water which flowed into the Dane around there, because of the mineral make-up of the neighbouring ground, could be used as a cure for witchcraft, the evil eye, if it was drunk for nine mornings on the trot. He added this was "an ample index to the minds of the inhabitants."

Gradbach mill when it was in a derelict state; now, it is a fine Youth Hostel.

Here, I wonder if it would be stretching a point too much to mention the significance of the number nine ... to the Celts this number was sacred. The Triple Goddesses were thrice three, there were nine mythological maidens in their stories and nine stones together symbolised the attendants of Bridgit, the fertility goddess, whose name is still kept alive at The Bridestones by Bosley Cloud, the Stones of Bridgit. Nine was also the mystical number associated with the rites of the Beltaine fires, for eighty one men attended these rites, nine times nine. Later, to the Christians, the all-powerful triad, the Father, Son and Holy Ghost, was the Triple Traid of nine making the whole, a holy and celestial number.

The Colour of the water that flows in the Dane, often brown and sometimes reddish, brings me on to another point mentioned to me by Frank Parker and this concerns Gradbach or The Great Bitch. Frank mentioned to me at one time the fact that there are gravestones in Flash (or Quarnford) churchyard that denote the place of the deceased as being "Great Bitch", or Gradbach. The usual theory of the derivation of the name Gradbach is that Bach is a stream, as in Sandbach, the sandy stream. However, there can be no doubt whatsoever that the area now known as Gradbach, and more specifically the hill known as Gradbach Hill, was at one point known as The Great Bitch, an obvious reference to the Earth Goddess, the Earth Mother or Mother Earth. Out of this Great Earth Mother there flows a stream of red that may well have given the illusion of suggestion of menstruation.

By the Forest Gate

The Rose and Crown at Allgreave (meaning hill on the corner) is, to me, a boundary of the Dane Valley. From there, on the main Congleton to Buxton Road we are in Forest and Clough territory, although in point of fact the Valley of the Dane used to be a part of the old hunting forest known as the Forest of Macclesfield. But anyway, for the point of this exercise the Valley of the Dane is just that.

I can never really bring myself to call this pub the Rose and Crown for, to me, it will always have an affectionate spot in my heart as "Jimmy's." I have many fond and happy memories of the colourful Cypriot Jimmy Panayi who was the jovial, and just ever so slightly eccentric, host of the hostelry in the late 60s and early 70s. He was the man who extended the place and converted a shippon at the side into a cosy dining area and he was a man who, unfortunately, passed away far too early in life. Here's to you, Jimmy. Today it is a public house I would recommend most heartily for its excellent food and an ambience second to none.

Let us take a journey along the road from the Rose and Crown, sign-posted for Quarnford, and into the real heart and soul of the Dane Valley. Past Pearls Farm, whose name remembers the "perlieu" or enclosure for animals (a remnant of the Forest) and where, close by, a strong earth line, dragon line or ley line, crosses over from the south towards the lowes of Rainow northward. On the left we come to Eagle and Child Cottage, once a public house of that name on what used to be the convergence of a pack horse trail from the valley and the road leading in to the hunting forest. The pub, now a cottage, gets its name from the coat of arms of the Stanleys or Derbys, stewards of the forest, for on the coat of arms there is depicted an eagle standing over a child in the nest. There are quite a few variations of stories given to account for this and one is that Sir John Stanley, about the time Edward III, married Isabella, daughter and heiress of Sir Thomas Lathom, of great possessions. Sir Thomas mourned that he had no son and one day found a child in an eagle's nest close by his stately mansion. He took it and said it was his natural son but Lady Stanley, in contempt and derision of the spurious brother, took the eagle and child for a crest in token of conquest over him and his claims. As likely as any of the stories but perhaps there is an element of truth in this for the eagle is the symbol of the liberated spirit and, perhaps, the crest symbolises the freedom the Stanleys and Derbys had over the rest of the people at that time because that baby is wrapped tightly in swaddling, perhaps a symbol of bondage.

Move on further into the valley towards the river and on the left is the road to Bennetsitch, a homely farmstead. In the 1960s and 70s it was the home of people I count as exceedingly good friends, Mike and Ella Oldham. It is Mike who I have to thank for introducing me to the secrets of dowsing and I am sure he wouldn't mind me telling the story of how we first met. For a time I had moved into town and Mike and Ella moved in next door but one on the same cul-de-sac. One evening he knocked on the front door of our Victorian home and Hilary, my wife, answered,

"Do you know about ley lines?" he asked, quite matter of fact.

And that was it. A former pupil of Freud, by the name of Jung, coined a word that fits that meaningful coincidence. It is synchronicity. By a meaningful coincidence coupled with intuition, Mike had been drawn to his near neighbours whom he had never met and knew nothing about but he instinctively knew that there, one house away, lived like-minded people. We have had a firm friendship ever since and he featured in my previous work when I wrote about the Line of Ley through Dieulacresse Abbey that was dowsed by myself, my son,

Charles, and Mike. This is the ley line that crosses the road near Pearls Farm a mere cock's stride from Bennetsitch.

Wincle, from an old photograph, looking up to the Ship Inn on the top right-hand side.

Just a trifle further along the road there is Midgley Gate, a softly coloured and gentle abode of ancient origins. It was very much a part of the old hunting forest and gets its name from the fact that it is by Midgley Hill (Midgley meaning big lea or meadow) and the Gate element from the road leading into the forest. It is thought that the farm was used to supply the royal hunters with food and, indeed, beasts for the chase.

Down the road and on the right we come to a residence that was once a curious hostelry nicknamed Peg Cottage, or Peg Inn. It was a house that sold ale to thirsty callers, but it did not possess a licence to do so, and it is said that the thirsty traveller could call at the building and purchase a peg which, by an amazing coincidence, just happened to be the price of the ale they craved. The proprietor of the Peg Inn would then give the purchaser of the peg a drink of ale for "free".

As the road swings to the right before crossing the River Dane there is a plaque on the left hand side, snuggling into the wall. It is in memory of the late Clifford Rathbone who for many years wrote articles for the

Macclesfield local paper, then called the County Express, under the nom de plume of "Stroller". His articles were about local history and they were also about the countryside he knew with intimate detail and passion. I had the great honour of being asked to unveil this plaque along with his widow, Doreen, after his untimely death in the early 1970s. I like to think that he and now Doreen who has joined with him again in some other place are once more strolling hand in hand around the Dane Valley, a land they both loved so dearly. I owe a lot to Clifford, for he taught me much and trusted me enough to allow me to inherit from him the editorship of his beloved Macclesfield newspaper.

As we continue our journey down the road, Gradbach Methodist Chapel, the Chapel in the Hills (although, in fact, it's in a valley), greets us on the left-hand side. Built in 1849 it was erected to serve the spiritual needs of the many families who lived thereabouts in those days; people who worked at Gradbach Mill, in the coalmines of Goldsitch Moss or the farms thereabouts. If we are to carry on, before we come to Old Ike's Cottage where the road bears over the bridge astride The Dane and up to The Moss and Royal Cottage, we come to a road on the right which takes us to the Scout Camp and the Youth Hostel, once Gradbach Mill. This old silk mill has many a tale to tell. It used to be the centre of a thread making industry run by power from a waterwheel on the Dane. It is said that a young girl was once trapped in the wheel and sadly crushed to death. As the wheel turned from then onwards, her cries could be heard. Close by is Manor House Farm, another scene of a supposed haunting. This is the building where, some 500 years ago or more the court of the forest lands used to be held and it has been said that the ghost of a man, thought to have been sentenced to death at the court, walks every full moon.

There are yet more "haunted" houses in the district. Swythamley Hall itself is, perhaps not surprisingly, rumoured to possess the ghost of a mistress of a member of the De Trafford family who walks the rooms, searching for the baby she lost during childbirth. And at Gradbach Hall, near to Hanging Stone there is said to be the spectre of a woman carrying a head, who emerges from one room where an infant died. There are, in point of fact, gravestones under the floor of a barn at this Hall and it could very well have been the site of a chapel, adjoining the house, at one point in history.

If it is more ghosts we crave then let us travel only a short way to the village of Wincle. This is the village that saw the might of Bonnie Prince

Charlie's army march past on the way to Leek and Derby; for then it was on the main route from Macclesfield to Leek, before the turnpike. One soldier, a little the worse for wear after calling at the Ship Inn left a gun and dagger at the public house, and these were on view to customers, certainly the last time I went in. It is past the Ship and down to the Dane that a headless horseman is supposed to ride on misty nights, and up in those parts there are many misty nights, with the clouds hanging low over the hills and in the valley. There was a church and chapel of ease at the site of the present church in the eleventh century, and from this ecclesiastical establishment there is one more of those time-honoured tales of underground passages leading to another ecclesiastical building, in this case Wincle Grange, which was a Cistercian Priory in the fourteenth century. The more I hear of the underground passages, which can never be discovered, the more I am convinced they allude to the earth lines, or ley lines, which the vast majority of these ancient religious sites are to be found on, where they, quite often, replaced existing pagan places.

The Ship Inn, which bears a picture of the ship that took Sir Philip Brocklehurst and Courtney Brocklehurst, then two young bucks of the Swythamley dynasty, to the South Pole, has a footpath leading from its northerly car park. This takes the walker into a wooded vale and then out to the fields of Bartomley Farm, where there is now a scheduled Ancient Monument, and so anyone found digging or treasure hunting will be in deep, deep trouble. It has been described as a Neolithic long barrow. It is here that there is the site of, what many people believe, was a huge battle many years ago. Between which armies there is no certainty, only obscurity, but in the 1870s some tenants of the Brockle-hurts of Swythamley discovered gold artifacts in a burial mound, part of which can still be seen, although much digging has now mis-shaped the site and it must be deduced this digging has not been altogether for archaeological purposes. The find is recorded in a book written by Sir Philip Brocklehurst entitled *Swythamley and its Neighbourhood* and published in 1874. In this he wrote: "At Bartomley, a Swythamley farm on the Cheshire side of the River Dane, in Wincle township, have at various times been discovered a considerable number of antiquities, consisting of gold rings, in one instance with a god or goddess engraved on the jewel, gold chains, with links of curious green stones called prez, together with gold ornaments considered to be bosses or shield ornaments, the last discovered being a very beautiful fibula of virgin gold. These things have usually been picked up, after the plough has disturbed the soil, on a steep bank resembling artificial earthworks, probably a Roman encampment, and at the foot of which, through a wooded ravine, flows the Dane." Rumour had it that there had been quite a number of other such finds over the years, but the Lord of the Manor had not been made aware of these and no doubt they were made good use of by his tenants.

In the year 1877 an inventory of all the finds was made and it showed:

a. A 22 inch long chain with eight small links made from greenstone and another chain, nine inches long but without stones.

b. A seven inch long piece of gold chain with 19 figure of eight links with an ornament at the end.

c. A "very massive and elegant" gold fibula.

d. A gold ring with a winged figure on the stone.

e. A highly ornamental gold ring with the stone missing.

f. Part of a very thin beaten gold mask with gold hair.

g. A number of gold beads and studs.

Two years later another thin piece of gold was unearthed. This was flat and had holes in the side through which gold wire passed, and it was thought at the time to be part of a breast ornament.

The late Gordon Rowley in his treatise *Macclesfield in Prehistory* said this "fibula" was a crossbow shaped brooch dating to the fourth century..D. He added that the figure on the ring was a cloaked female, and what was thought to be a mask which was "nothing more than a crumpled fragment of sheet gold." He said they were the personal jewellery of a Roman or a Romano Briton and possibly belonging to this person's wife as well.

The owner of the farm in the 1970s is recorded as having expressed the belief of many local people that this is the site of a fierce battle, and the remains of the vanquished are at rest under the soil thereabouts.

When my good friend Maurice Winnell spoke to the farmer one day he was told there was a "stone circle" just up the way that "everyone seems to pass by." Maurice registered it and filed it away in his memory for investigation at a future time and, I am pleased to say, chose one autumn afternoon in 1992 when he and I were investigating the "burial site" at Bartomley. He mentioned what the farmer had said to him and so, after making a thorough inspection of the Ancient Monument and having taken pictures for posterity, we decided to have a look for this "stone circle", not knowing what to expect. We followed the path that leads through the farm yard and walked along for a matter of a few hundred yards up a slight incline.

Maurice Winnell at the Ancient Monument site at Bartomley Farm. It is very overgrown and there is much evidence of excavation.

There on the left-hand side was the definite outline of a stone circle some forty feet across. A "circle" is not in fact the correct description, it is more of an oval and those stones that are not overgrown with grass are some two or three feet high. All, that is, save for one which has toppled over or had been toppled over at some time. This is more like five and a half feet in length or height. This stone circle is worthy of much more investigation now that it has been rediscovered. It does lie on private property to the left of the path and so this will most definitely have to be borne in mind should any one wish to visit there, but it is easily viewed from the public footpath. There looks as though there may very well have been some sort of processional way from this circle to the burial mound where the gold ornaments were found, and it does not take great powers of deduction to realise the two sites were most definitely connected, if not by a processional way then most certainly by the earth knowledge of those who have gone before. The circle is virgin territory as it were and there is much detail to be taken in. Perhaps we may meet there one fine day, who knows.

The stone circle or oval at Bartomley Farm, Wincle, is overgrown and proves difficult to visualise from a photograph, but with the aid of an artist outlining the photograph the picture becomes clearer.

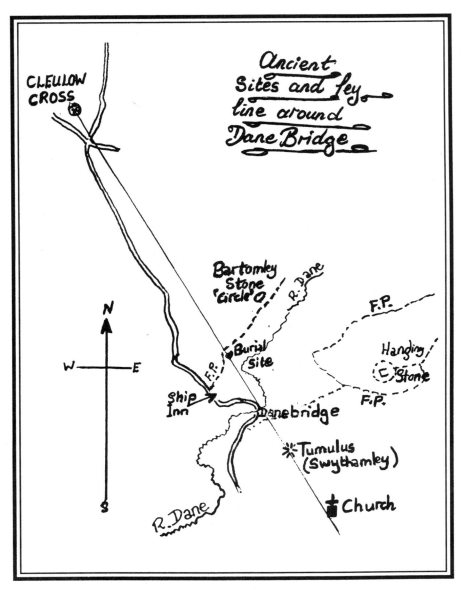

A plan showing an earth line on the sites of Swythamley Church, the tumulus, the burial site and Cleulow Cross.

A stone pillar presumably once upright and now lying in the field at the site of the stone circle or oval.

5

LAND OF THE HIGH ROCKS

Rocks of Baal

High above the valley wherein nestles the Queen of the Moorlands, the gentle township of Leek, there is an expanse of rock, the southerly tip of the Pennine Range. When the French holy men who were monks of the Cistercian Order came to the Abbey of Dieulacres, they looked up and saw the crags and called them, not unnaturally,"the rocks". In French this is the Roaches, sometimes written as Roches and whilst not being very romantic in their name, they are as beautifully formed as a Shakespearian sonnet, as domineering as doom and as full of history as the British Museum. They are special in so many ways; as a geological outcrop they are unique and as a remembrance of the old ways they are an open book.

In this tract of land, which stretches from Tittesworth Reservoir, Meerbrook and Upperhulme in the south to Axe Edge and Flash in the north, there are many memories of those who have gone before, as well as memorials to gods and God and a lingering of practices that have been suppressed over many centuries but have by no means died. Mists of time hang in the air unmoved by winds of change, and the gods of the ancients and traditions of men of old are kept alive within the rocks, the soil and the peat, re-generating in the purple heather and the bilberries that abound, kept alive in the cry of the curlew and still riding on the breezes that can so easily turn to deadly gales.

There was a forest on these high crags many hundred of years ago. A forest that was home to the oak, the rowan, the ash and the beech. A forest of trees that was home to the wolf, the boar, the bear the wildcat and the wild men. And, as now, those stones lay on the ground, carried down by the mammoth glaciers of the Ice Age, or so the historians and geologists would tell us. Others have believed they were carried there by the gods. In those far off days they were huge boulders hiding within the vast tracts of trees or in a clearing within the greenery. Every now and then the skyline would be met by a high rock jutting above the tree tops: a high rock like the Hen Cloud, sitting as a broody fowl on her chicks or like Ramshaw Rocks, a clearing within a wood wherein rams roamed. To the north there is Adders Green, where the snakes abounded in the lush grassland to the side of the forest. To the south the forest extended for many miles; part of the Forest of Leek stewarded by the Davenports who were also in charge of the Forest of Macclesfield; these two woodlands combining to juxtapose with the Forest of Lyme – that huge dividing forest, the merkland, that isolated the Earldom of Chester from the world.

The Bawd Stone, a boulder venerated by the ancients for its healing properties and later looked upon as something evil.

Walkers from Leek pause by the Bawdstone in the 1930s (Mr and Mrs Pace).

In a field by the road that lies underneath The Roaches, only a stride or two away from the Bawd Stone, there is this stone pillar some twenty feet or so away from the boulder pictured in the background. The two align exactly on the winter solstice.

And over the centuries the wood became coal and men would start to dig it for their fires and furnaces, just as they had chopped the wood for the same purpose many years before. Hundreds of families moved in to mine the coal; many lived in crude makeshift huts, some lived in shelters by the side of rocks and others built small homes from stone hewn from the rocks and dug from the ground. But before the miners moved in, men and women would eke out a living from the soil, a few sheep perhaps and goats providing their income and their food. Some who lived on the high ground cut amulets from the rocks as protection from the evil spirits and the townsfolk would eagerly buy these body ornaments to ward off the evil eye, the wyrd ones (oft-times called witches) and the bogarts and demons. These same purveyors of amulets used the thick soil, enriched with peat and loam and all many of minerals to shape into charms also used to protect the holder.

Among the many thousand of rocks and stones that abound in the Land of the High Rocks there are three which were among the Special Ones in days departed, although it must be said these were Special in days of not so long ago as well. That which went before is still kept alive in names handed down to us, if in nothing more. First in the trio of wyrd sisters is the Bawd Stone, a healing stone that was – falsely it would appear – classed as evil. Second is the Ballstone or Baal's Stan at Ballstone Farm, a site of Beltaine Fires, and the final one of the triumvirate is the Baldstone at Baldstone Farm, where midsummer ceremonies of the mistletoe were held.

Let us look more closely. The Bawdstone is technically a glacial erratic rock, carried down by a glacier and left standing some eighteen inches to two feet above the ground, perched atop some smaller rocks. *A Guide of Footpaths on The Roaches and Hen Cloud* published by Staffordshire Moorlands District Council says it has been described as a burial chamber, and adds that most such explanations had "evil connotations", and then mentioned the custom early in the twentieth century of whitewashing the stone. Unfortunately it does not mention who actually referred to this stone as evil and created the practice of whitewashing it, a symbol of good over bad. I think in this instance the "bad" part of the stone has been the fact that it has been used for un-Christian practices, and those were related to healing. There is a tradition among local people, quite a number of others are aware of it, that this strange stone was looked upon as a "good" stone; a stone that was used to make people well. The people of Leek and surrounding areas, extending I am told to Buxton and beyond, and certainly up until the time of the Second World War (and, who knows, probably to this day) brought sick people to that stone and made them clamber underneath it and out the other side, to "knock the devil from their backs." Anyone who has actually crawled underneath this huge boulder (and my dear wife and I can count ourselves among them) will tell you that it is a tight squeeze and your back is indeed scraped. There is a well defined path from Leek through Upperhulme and Tittesworth that goes straight to the Bawd Stone, and this must mean that the route was well used for centuries upon centuries. It is not just a footpath, is a trackway and was thus a route used considerably. It is a trackway that leads directly to the Bawdstone, defined by the thousands upon thousands of weary feet that have tramped their ways along it in the past in the hope of being healed. This healing stone was used not because it was capable of being crawled under (that came later when tradition clouded fact) but because it contained healing properties. Those properties are still there, I might add, if you wish to find them and may have something to do with the high quartz content of the rock coupled with the powerful earth energy line the Bawd Stone is upon.

So why has it the name "Bawd" Stone? It may possibly stem from the same source as "bawdy" meaning indecent or it may come from the old French *baude* meaning a procuress. This is interesting because if so it shows two points very strikingly. The first is that it probably received the name from the French monks at nearby Dieulacres Abbey, who farmed at Roach Grange, and the second is that it refers to the feminine aspect of the rock which takes us to earth worship, and that means Mother Earth, the female goddess. Slightly north there is a rock dedicated to Balder, the Scandinavian and Anglo Saxon god of vegetation who could also be the female goddess venerated as Mother Earth as Frig, Freya and Balder. Frig is still used as a connotation of the "bawdy" four-letter word to this day. So perhaps Bawd Stone and Bald Stone have the same origin. Or perhaps "bawd" is a colloquial form of "bad". Looking north east of Bawd Stone, on the exact bearing of sunrise at the Summer Solstice there is a hill by the name of Summer Hill, which could well place this rock in the realms of something more than just a healing rock, although there is a distinct possibility that the sun's rays at the summer solstice descending on the Bawd Stone would have had a decidedly potent effect on those assembled. Slightly over a mile south of the Bawd Stone there is a tumulus (SK06/16:648-003), an ancient, possibly neolithic, burial mound that adds weight to the theory that the area was something rather special.

North of the Bawd Stone and Summerhill there is a farm called Baldstone, which used to be in the possession of the Bowyer family before the Second World War. This is in the area known as Hazelbarrow, the name now used for a fish farm and boarding kennels of repute. The appendage "barrow" must surely denote an ancient burial and is close by to Newstone, where a chapel was placed at the side of the farm because, it is said, of the pagan ways of those who lived in the neighbourhood. This was a few hundred years ago and there is no record, as far as I am aware, of when it was actually erected although it did cease as a chapel in the 1920s.

Baldstone possibly derives its name from Balder as well. Balder was a Norse or Viking god, the son of Odin. Balder was slain by a branch of mistletoe and he was burnt, says the legend, in a huge fire. Mistletoe was, as we have already discussed, sacred to the Druids and Pliny said of mistletoe: "The Druids, for so they call their wizards, esteem nothing more sacred than the mistletoe and the tree on which it grows, provided only that the tree is an oak. But apart from this they choose oak-woods for their sacred groves and perform no sacred rites without oak leaves." He describes the ceremony in which a priest in a white robe climbs a tree and cuts the mistletoe with a golden sickle and catches it in a white cloth. Then they sacrifice victims. They also believed barren animals would bring forth with a potion of mistletoe and the plant was a remedy against all poison. The plant was called the all-healer and, in the eyes of the Druids, if the plant was cut at Midsummer's Eve or Midsummer Day it induced dreams of omen (here I refer again to Summer Hill close by). But to return to Balder. When he died thanks to the mistletoe plant, his body was burnt on a pyre and this was dedicated in the Balefires (Balder's Balar which were huge fires lit at Midsummer, part of a ceremony to make the sun continue to shine. These fires were fuelled by human victims who were supposed to be embodiments of tree spirits or vegetation for Balder was the fertility god of vegetation.)

And now we must travel less than a mile to the third of the Stones. This is Ball Stone, the stone of Baal, another stone connected with the gods of old and with the burning of fires. Ballstone Farm is now a thriving mushroom farm owned by two delightful people, Mr and Mrs Frank Parker. Curiously enough, my wife Hilary and I first had the pleasure of meeting them around a midsummer fire, but on this occasion it was a happy barbecue, far removed from the Beltaine Fires that once burned brightly on the Land of the High Rocks. The Ball Stone is another of those curious rock formations that abound on The Roaches. It is perched, precariously it appears, on the top of others. I went along to Ball Stone Farm to photograph the stone and Frank showed me traces of charcoal and burnt coal in a crevice under the rock. This was extremely old, but of what age exactly it is impossible for me to hazard even a guess. It may have been burnt by the itinerant tinkers who wandered thereabouts and who sheltered under the rocks (they have more than a passing connection with the notorious Flashmen or Flash Coiners and may even have been responsible for the title and the tradition – *Myths and Legends of East Cheshire & The Moorlands*). The charcoal and ashes could have had something to do with a group of people who came to the area to mine coal and who pitched their home wherever they could, and wherever shelter would be found. It could be something to do with the Beltaine Fires.

So what were these Fires of Baal, and who was Baal? The Bale Fires would, at one point in our history, have been burnt at the changing of the four seasons of the year to commemorate the sun passing through the heavens and we journey, yet again, to the myths and the practices of the Druids to look further. This god Baal or Bel later was changed to Beelzebub by the Christians and the Priests of Baal in the Bible carried out human sacrifices by throwing their victims into a fire.

The stones of Baal at Ballstone Farm, courtesy F. Parker.

Baal's origins are in the Middle East, possibly Palestine, and he was the Bull god who wore horns and was the husband of Astarte who became Diana. The Bullstone at Cleulow Cross in Macclesfield Forest has the same derivation of name, and is connected through the fire worship of Baal to keep the seasons in their rightful order and also is associated with Baal the Bull. The four seasonal times when the Beltaine Fires were, and still are, burnt, were the festivals of the Druids and May 1st, a traditional fertility celebration when the phallus maypole is danced around is known as Beltaine. Writing in 1769, Thomas Pennant, a traveller through Celtic Scotland said that on 1st May the herdsmen of every village held their Bel-tien, a rural sacrifice. They cut a hole in the turf and made a fire and cooked cakes of oatmeal.

The 'Winking Man' on The Roaches. Once venerated by the ancients, but now a local saying asks: How did the Winking Man lose an eye? Because he saw a virgin walk past from Leek and he blinked so much through the shock of it that it blinded him! Other variations are best left to the imagination. Celtic gods had the habit of closing one eye.

Close by the Winking Man are these markings on a small boulder embedded in the ground. I rubbed peat into the carvings to ensure they showed up on the photograph. Each is about eighteen inches in length. There is a possibility that Thor's hammer could be the hammer of Woden instead. At Biddulph Parish Church, some ten or so miles away to the south, where there are tombstones said to be of Crusaders, there are markings of the Knight's Templar straight sword. On one there is a Crusader cross surmounted on Woden's world ash, or hammer, which is perhaps symbolic of the union of Christianity and Woden's pagan earth cult. The hammer and the cross look very familiar.

Each person would break off one ninth and throw it on the fire "for the preservation of my horse" then another piece for the preservation of another animal and so on. Another writer described an eighteenth century ritual whereby boiled milk and eggs, a custard, is made and eaten with special cakes, presumably consecrated cakes cooked on the Beltaine fires. This cake had knobs on it and pieces would be broken off and it is supposed this tradition stems from the manner in which the victim of the fire used to be chosen. Whosoever broke off the chosen piece fed the flames. On older maps of the Roaches a field below the great rocks and just north of Tittesworth is shown as Custard Field. A tradition survived in the not too dim and distant past of rolling cakes down hills at Beltaine and it is presumed this was, previously, an act whereby wheels of fire (possibly barrels of flaming tar) were rolled down hills. It has often been said that Kerridge Hill where White Nancy now stands was such a hill for the Beltaine fires.

I also owe thanks to Frank Parker for putting me on to the trail of a two marks in a rock on the Roaches which were certainly worthy of investigation, close by the famous rock called "The Winking Man". The Winking Man is a rock some ten feet in height that juts out of Ramshaw Roaks overlooking the Leek to Buxton Road. Its formation is for all the world that of a man's face with a forehead, eyes, nose, mouth and chin. The traveller on the old Roman road going past the Winking Man sees the eye "wink" because the changing angle and the stones to the back of it give the effect of the eye opening and closing. The nose on this peculiar formation was much more pronounced at one time but some kind person decided to vandalise it in the 1970s, I believe, and the nose is not now as noticeable as it used to be. But there is no doubt whatsoever that to our forefathers back in the days when any natural structure was a trifle unusual, therefore super-natural, this was some-thing special and was most probably assumed to be the face of a god, possibly Thor or Woden. A clue to this lies in the markings a little way away that Frank pointed out to me.

The stone face known as the Winking Man can be seen very easily, but to get close to it is a little more difficult. The pathways do not lead directly to the rock structure, but around it and the heather often hides little (and larger) traps for the unwary in the form of holes in the ground. But there is a well-defined path which has been made easy to traverse by the efforts and spadework of the Peak Park Rangers which goes pretty near to it. On this path, just to the south of the structure, there is a stone embedded into the earth and on this a Christian cross is carved, alongside a hammer, presumably the Hammer of Thor or Thunor, the god of thunder. The cross looks to be slightly younger in age than the hammer, which may mean the hammer of Thor was on its own at one time and the rock was made holy by the addition of the cross. However, they could equally, have both been carved at the same time. They have both been carved to a depth of half and inch or so and the weathering shows they have both been on the rock for a considerable while. The proximity to the face on the rock close by may, of course, be co-incidental but personally I think not.

There is much to explore on The Roaches, and I would recommend anyone who has never been to certainly try to visit the area, if only for an hour or so. There are countless stories told of the mist-covered rocks and the people who have inhabited them. There has, supposedly, been a group of Vikings or Danes resident there in the past and many strangely shaped stones have been called sacrifice stones or Druids' stones. I think that all the tales result from an awareness of what used to be but this awareness has been clouded, not only by the mists of time but by the inadequacies of the mind. Undoubtedly a great number of un-Christian happenings have been taken place there, and it is said that the chapel at the area of land known as Hazelbarrow (itself a spot where a barrow, or ancient earthwork, was sited) was placed there to counter the goings-on of the populace. This chapel was placed on to the side of Newstone Farm and could accommodate twenty or thirty people at the most. It closed in the 1920s and records go back to the year 1820 although it was most certainly there before that time. In the year 1820 it was described as an "unpretentious building" with plain pews in four rows.

On Hen Cloud, or End Cloud or Hern's Cloud (Cloud meaning hill), there is a cairn which shows Neolithic Man venerated the area and close by is the dew pond known as Doxey Pool. This lakelet, at an altitude of 1,500 feet, is supposedly connected to the Mermaid's Pool at Morridge. A mermaid has been sighted at Doxey Pool, as well as other fabulous creatures. "Doxey" could refer to the Anglo Saxon pronunciation of oxen, therefore the oxen's pool, or it could be named after a local family, still in the area, called Doxey. The name also colloquially refers to a lady of easy virtue, perhaps the mermaid. The pool never seems to increase or decrease in size, the water is always very cold and very clear and no animals are said to drink from it. Just like the Morridge pool, no birds are supposed to fly over it.

Perhaps we can return to the Bawd Stone for a little while, because there is an extremely interesting treatise on this magical stone which was written for the North Staffs Field Club's annual report of 1913 to 1914 by A.M. McAldowie, M.D., F.R.S., and accompanying it is a photograph of the stone actually painted white. I came across this text quite by chance the very day after I had written the preceding piece on the Bawdstone, Ballstone and Baldstone. I was in the reference section of Leek Library and decided to check if there was anything written about any of the Stones, and this jumped out at me, not literally but as near as damn it.

The first reference book I laid my hands upon opened at a page that made a cross reference to the Bawd Stone.

The Caledonian doctor wrote that the first visit he made to the Bawd Stone was in 1879 in company with a Mr R. Hardley, who informed him that during his boyhood a "gathering of the people" from the farms and cottages of the surrounding district took place at this spot each May Day, when the stone was whitewashed with "some ceremony". The Doctor went on to write that the capping stone of the "monument" as he termed the Stone is mounted just high enough to allow one to crawl underneath. The space below, therefore, probably formed a sacred "Creep Way" and had been connected with certain religious rites in ancient times.

He goes on to quote that until the middle of the nineteenth century, it was the custom for several thousand people of all ages and both sexes to assemble on 23rd December at the festival of St Declan on the strand at Ardmore Bay, Ireland. The men crawled under the holy rocks and then struck their backs three times against the stone. The date of the festival indicated it had been originally held at the winter solstice and therefore connected with sun worship.

Doctor McAldowie paid a visit to the Bawd Stone to find out whether it had any astronomical relationship. He wrote: "It stands on the western ridge of the Roaches on the part where the range forks into an eastern and a western branch. This bifurcation (division into two) gives the high eastern horizon employed by the ancients to get a clear view of the rising sun. There is no standing stone, tumulus or other artificial object now in existence marking the position of sunrise on the date of any pagan festivals. The ancients, however, often made use of some pro- minent natural feature in the landscape for this purpose, and one of the favourite points employed was where the line of the horizon is broken by the intersection of two ranges of hills. Now, at the east-north-east of this megalith, at the place of sunrise about the beginning of May, there is such an intersection and it is the most strongly marked and definite point on the line of the horizon. Astronomy thus supports the view that this monument was an ancient altar or "sun stone".

Not only were such stones themselves anointed and considered sacred, but the tracks of land on which they stood, whether they were enclosed or open, were sanctuaries or holy places. The gods were not thought to be omnipotent, but merely super-human beings ..."

Here he delves into conjecture on how the ceremony would be performed. He wrote: "The ceremony began at sunrise as the god had to be present at the sacrifice and consisted of a procession round, probably three times. Fossae (ditches) surrounding stone circles, avenues of standing stones ... are regarded as evidences that sacred processions formed part of the ceremonial at ancient pagan festivals. Numerous instances are recorded in works on folklore of the practice of walking three times around prehistoric monuments from east to west according to the course of the sun. This sanctified tour is supposed to be a survival of the ancient religious processions. Always with the procession was the ritual of passing through the sacred creep-way. The animal appointed for sacrifice was then slain, its blood poured or sprinkled over the stone and its flesh eaten by the worshippers. Three months later at the beginning of August the sun on its journey south again rises at the same point of the horizon."

There is a footnote to this tract, which reads: "The Rev. W. Beresford in a paper *Celtic and Druids* (transactions of the North Staffs Field Club, 1884, p. 24) says the Bawd Stone is a corrupt form of Balderson or Baal Stone of the Sun God."

So there we have some interesting points about the Stone. The confirmation of the ceremony at May Day is tremendous, and the fact that the Doctor looked at alignments with the sun as long ago as the early years of the twentieth century, before computerised theories of alignments were the vogue, is quite startling. What he did not give credit to the Stone for, of course, is the healing properties that those who used its powers gained from it, or hoped they would gain from it. He implies that the Stone was moved there by man, and does not delve into the glacial drift theories at all. Perhaps the stone was moved to the place, for it is rather a coincidence that it has alignments with the spring and summer equinoxes. Nature is not usually accidentally exact and if it was placed there by man then we can deduce that the alignment with the solstice was so that extra power could be gained; if the stone was purely a marker for the equinox then it was an incredibly large and cumbersome object to use. A stone pillar would have been more exact and a darn sight easier.

A farm and area called Summer Hill less than a mile away is on the line of the spring and summer equinox from the Stone. This name occurs again on the same bearing at Fools Nook (Grove of the Ancients) and at Morridge with Merryton Low where it is an area, and now a farm, that goes by the name of Noon Sun. On the same bearing, north-north-east, from Ballstone Farm where both the spring and summer equinox lie there is yet another Summer Hill. This is at Flash Bar. We do not know of course that these Summer Hills and the Noon Sun are related to the sacred sites, which were used as ceremonies to the summer sun, but the coincidence is quite remarkable.

The walk to the Bawd Stone from the minor road which skirts the base of the Roaches is a pleasant one. What is instantly noticeable, if you can keep your eyes from wandering over the magnificent views, or your ears from listening to the cries of the grouse or the song of the wind, is the number of standing stones either still upright in the ground, recumbent on the heather and grass or utilised into the drystone walls. I was told by a very experienced hiker that these stones are nothing to do with anything ancient, they are merely scratching posts for the sheep. What a load of old cobblers. Would any farmer in those wild and windswept

moors spend probably the best part of one or two days shaping the stones, carting them to a handy spot for the sheep and then erecting them in the ground, to a depth of some three of four feet so his flock could have a good scratch? Assuming he would, then they were the best cared-for sheep in the land and the farmer had nothing better to occupy his time. No, these stones have been placed in the ground for another purpose, perhaps as markers for the ceremonial way to the sacred stone or perhaps as boundary markers. Maybe they were placed in the ground as sighting points.

One of what used to be three boundary stones just above Flash Bar (named after the toll bar at the turnpike) The stone is on a mound which may be a tumulus.

As I parked my car on that road beneath the High Rocks and prepared my camera and all the paraphernalia before walking to the Bawd Stone on a bright but cold winter's morn, I noticed a rock similar in size to the Bawd Stone on the southern side of that road, away from the Roaches. In front of this boulder some twenty feet away I noticed one of the "scratching posts" some three and a half feet tall and obviously chiselled with care and affection. The compass showed the boulder and the standing stone to be lined up with the winter equinox, the exact opposite to the Bawd Stone which lies over the ridge and higher up among the rocky crags. Another coincidence perhaps, or then again, perhaps not.

At the Bawd Stone there is discernible a circular path which, if the theory of the processional way and the perambulation clockwise or anticlockwise is correct, would tie in rather nicely. There seems to be no other reason for this path other than to circle the stone. Another well defined path leads to the stone. It goes nowhere else and would be rather odd and out of place if this stone had no special significance. Why should a path lead to a boulder in the middle of a field and then stop? I won't insult your intelligence by supplying what I feel is the obvious answer.

The Rush and the Hounds

Nestling below the high rocks of the Roaches there is the eerily silent valley wherein few noticeable remains of a once proud Cistercian Abbey are lying. This Abbey called Dieulacresse or Dieulacres lies next to a cave wherein an anchorite or hermit lived. I have referred to this area of wonders before; looking at a ley line that goes through the site and searching in the nooks and crannies of the cave (*Myths and Legends* book). But just north of this spot there is a wood that goes by the name of Hillswood and it is remarkable for a number of reasons, not least that it contains a healing tree. This tree (I will not identify it for good reason, there being a few evil people who would be intent on destruction if I should do so) is special to a number of good people who have realised its natural potential. I was told of this wonder by someone who has become a special friend. This person is a very well known public figure and, for that reason, I do not feel able to identify him or her in this context at the moment. One day, I am certain, that special person will want to be named but the time is not right.

The area above the Abbey, towered over by the Roaches, is also the Land of the Rush. Many locals have experienced The Rush and it is something that, once experienced, will never be forgotten. It is a gust of wind or, perhaps more accurately, the dispersal of the air as invisible forces rush by. This Rush is heard, it is also felt and, further, it is seen as grass, branches, clothing, or anything in its wake is moved as it goes by. These forces are, it is said, the re-enactment of numerous demons hurrying to claim the body of a nobleman. I will explain. The nobleman is or was Earl Randle, the ruler of the Earldom of Chester who was responsible for founding the Abbey, transferring the white canons or monks from Pulton to a safe haven in the boundary Forest of Lyme, away from the marauding Welsh. This was our spot below the Roaches. His grandfathers had told him, in a vision: "Go to Cholpedsdale, which is in the territory of Leake and in that place wherein of old was built a chapel in honor the Blessed Mary, Virgin, thou shalt found an abbey of the Order of the White Monks ... and it shall be a joy for thee and many others who shall be saved through that place. For on that same site must be erected a ladder whereby the prayers of angels ascend and descend and the vows of the men shall be offered to God: and let them give thanks, and over that place shall the name of the Lord be invoked with constant prayer."

The area "wherein of old was built a chapel in honor of the Blessed Mary" is thought to be a part of the township of Leek now known as Ladydale. Here there is a stone referred to as a plague stone and there is also, in the area, a number of tumulus (in the region of Birchall) which were, locally, known as Sheba's Breasts.

According to the "Percy Folio" the Earl was a man of many pious deeds that are said to have saved his soul after death. There is told the legend that when Earl Randle lay dying, a man of Wallingford observing numerous demons hurrying was told they were hastening to his death bed to accuse the Earl of his sins. These demons decided the Earl should be banished to the pain of eternal fire but the mastiff dogs, the huge hunting hounds kept by the Abbot and his underlings for hunting the deer in the forest, and many other dogs housed with them in the kennels barked "without stint." The area around the Abbey of Dieulacresse was filled with so loud a clamour that the Prince of the Demons, the Devil, in disgust ordered the Earl should be expelled from the domain of the Prince of Darkness, he proving to be such a great enemy of evil. In that way, the legend goes, Earl Randle was saved from hell by the eternal deafening barking of the Abbey hunting dogs.

Earl Randle is said to have died at Swythamely Hall, once a hunting lodge and later a stately home (said to be the place where Gawain stayed whilst in search of the Green Knight in that epic saga set in the North Midlands, Wales and The Wirral). In his will he provides for his heart to be buried at Swythamley and tradition had it that his body was buried at Dieulacres. Why he should have such an affection for the area, on the furthest easterly outpost of his personal empire, is not mentioned. Perhaps it may have been for the self same reason that another chieftain, some two thousand years before the Norman Earl's death, chose to be buried at Swythamley. In the grounds to this day can be seen a tumulus or burial ground, which for centuries had a stone marker on its peak. A special spot indeed.

The Rush, that phenomenon experienced by numerous people around the area to this day, is said to be those demons rushing to claim a soul for their master. The original soul they endeavoured to claim was that belonging to Earl as he lay on his deathbed at Swythamley, and the woodland of Hillswood is directly between Swythamley and Dieulacresse. I personally know people who say they have felt, seen and heard The Rush, one being knocked to the floor by its ferocity. I have also met a person who is convinced he has heard the Hounds one cold winter's morn as he walked the field skirting the ancient woodland.

By the Black Hag

The countless walkers who frequent The Roaches, especially now the National Trust has taken the area under its wings, invariably pass a signpost which says "Ann Roach" and if they follow the path they are taken by a farm, to the north west of the main rocks. A number of farmsteads took the name of the area on which they were built and this could well be the case here, with the entire area being known as Ann Roach. Although it may possibly have been the name of a character who once lived in the area it is more of a possibility that the name means the Rock Anu, of An, Aine or Ainne. The nearby River Dane is named after the Goddess Dana or Danu (as is the mighty River Danube) and likewise the River Dean that flows through Bollington and on to Wilmslow. The name Danu or Dana is also referred to as Anu or Ana and the Celtic tribe who took their name from this goddess – the Tuatha De Danaan (the tribes of the goddess Dana) – should really be the De Annan or the people of Anu.

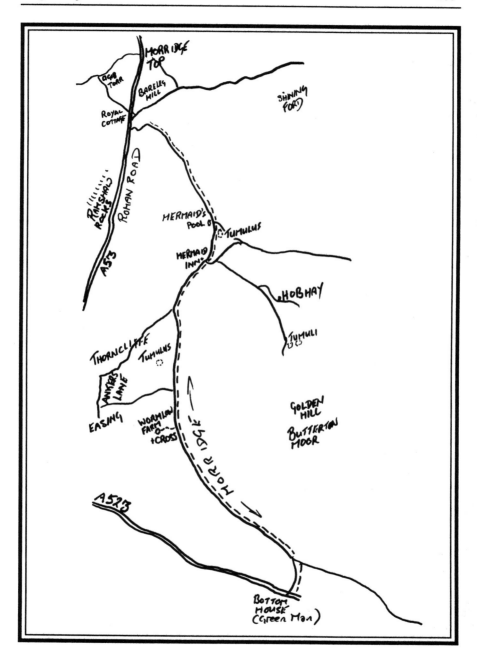

This area, therefore, may well mean Anu's Rock, the rock of the Earth Goddess. This deity Anu (even sometimes known as Briganta from where the Bridestones on Bosley Cloud, viewable from the Roaches, derive their name) was a goddess of the terrain, the earth just as Arnemetiae was a goddess of water, enshrined at nearby Buxton and Christianised as St Ann, hence St Ann's Well. In folklore tradition this Celtic earth goddess was changed into Black Anis, a child-eating ancient hag who had claws made from iron. Whenever there was a major catastrophe or a great emergency, most especially when a war was imminent, the goddess Anu in the form of an image, a statue, was paraded around a field atop a chariot that was known as the Anoniredi. Next to her, or her image, was the Consort: a sacrificial victim who would become her Consort at the split second point of the sacrifice, when his body was separated from his spirit.

On our Land of the Roaches there are rocks named after the Sun God and there are rocks named after the Earth Mother. There are rocks venerated for their healing and there are rocks at which fires were lit for the gods. In the chapter within this book on the Valley of the Dane, so closely intertwined with The Roaches, we see that there are also rocks used to ward off evil and some more hills named after Earth Goddess, in this case The Great Bitch.

Ridgeway of the Ancients

There is an ancient ridgeway, older than the Romans and later used by the packhorsemen whose commerce criss-crossed the entire Pennine Range, which goes by the name of "Morridge" or the Moor Ridgeway. It is well worthy of a moment or two's reflection.

These ridgeways or park horse trails are not unusual in the highlands of Cheshire, Derbyshire and Staffordshire. They, in the main, crossed from west to east, taking salt and other wares (from the Welsh and from the English ports) but there were some which traversed from north to south. One, which can still be mapped going through Pott Shrigley was supposedly the busiest in the country at one time, the M6 motorway of its day. It is hard now to imagine what sort of people used these trails. They were certainly hard and rugged and they could, there is no doubt, fend for themselves because there was always the chance of being set upon by the highway robbers – not the Dick Turpin types who wore black eye masks and sported duelling pistols, but the opportunists who took it upon themselves to have a go out on the bleak and desolate moorland, away from any law enforcers. But law enforcers there most certainly were. There were the packhorsemen themselves who would not think twice about using any defence they could, whether it was a pack of savage dogs so often accompanying the train of mules and trained to be as vicious as they cared to be, or a musket (always primed with powder and ball, just in case). Then of course there was the quarterstaff, a hefty fist or whatever. And who was to know what became of the would-be thieves? There was always a bog, a dew pond or a pack of hungry dogs to destroy the evidence, should evidence ever be sought.

But there was official law enforcement as well, however primitive. Each road went through a parish and each parish was legally responsible for guarding the trails and keeping them free from wrongdoers and, of course, collecting the pontage and portage (a penny or two from each packhorse train for going over a bridge or along a certain sections of the trail). Parish Constables were appointed and they, like the jaggers or packhorsemen, had their own ways of keeping the peace – and of warning would-be thieves. One of these ways, with the backing of the Crown up until the eighteenth century, was to "hang 'em high". A lofty peak or a rocky outcrop that could be viewed from all the roads in the vicinity would be chosen to have a gallows or gib atop. Any highway robbers or, indeed, any thieves, murderers and even poachers, who had the misfortune of being caught in that particular area stood a very good chance of being suspended from the gib, their bodies left there for as long as the bones and sinews lasted, usually two to three weeks, perhaps sooner if the carrion crows or the hawks were particularly hungry, as would have been the case more often than not in the winter time. The body was left as an example, or warning, to others.

Trails went across Goldsitch Moss by the side of the Roaches and emerged by the Roman Road later to be turnpiked between Leek and Buxton. And anyone who traversed this land, for about a mile or so around, could not fail to see an outcrop of rocks which still to this day carries the name Gib Tor (gibbet hill). Look closely atop the highest rock today and there is still evidence of where the gib used to be. A nearby farm callèd, not surprisingly, Gib Tor and once the show farm of the Harpur Crewe Estate was, incidentally, once said by the public health department of the old Leek Urban District Council to have the "sweetest tasting water in England", its water supply rising some half a mile north from a spring and running across Goldsitch Moss to Join the Dane. The road that passes Gib Tor Farm today from the main road close by Royal Cottage, a quaint and quite wonderful public house, is the road that Bonnie Prince Charlie took on his retreat from Derby towards Manchester. Tradition has it that he stayed the night at the country house now called Royal Cottage, but it is more likely that he stopped for refreshment (he was certainly a person who enjoyed a tipple or two). A nearby field is called Bareleg Hill and whereas this is usually the nickname given to an unproductive piece of land, according to John Field, who compiled *English Field Names*, local tradition has it that it is so called because of the barelegged, or kilted, Scottish soldiers who encamped there. Carry on from the road, Gib Tor Farm and past the gibbet rock and the traveller comes to Ballstone Farm where the owner, a wonderful chap by the name of Frank Parker who runs a mushroom farm there, once found a Scottish soldier's hat when he was digging in a nearby peat field. This cap was well preserved and still contained the piece of cloth which clans wore to identify themselves, although it was stained too much for the colours to be made out. The hat was given to Stafford Museum.

Morridge, the ridgeway across the moor, is a perfect example of these trails of long ago and it is still in use today as a thoroughfare. In the main it begins in the north at Morridge Top where there is a farm of the same name and, round Bareleg Hill and Royal Cottage (from where other trails radiate) goes southwards to Bottom House, where the sign of the Green Man still hangs at the pub at the crossroads and from Waterfall on to Waterhouses and along the old Earlsway (the way of the Earls of Chester) to Ashbourne and beyond. It is most certainly possible the trail went through Waterfall, past the village cross. Look on the map and it is easy to see that this was part of a trail at the very least from Manchester to Derby.

But what I would like to explore along this route is not the geographical lay of the land, although the views are breathtaking and well worth more than just a quick look, but the wealth of ancient and mystical evidence that still remains. From Royal Cottage southwards, our first stop is by the dew pool officially called Blake Mere and traditionally known as the Mermaid's Pool (O.S. sheet 119 SJ 0461). I mentioned in my previous book *Myths and Legends of East Cheshire and the Moorlands*, that this is probably a corruption of Mere or Meer Maid but now perhaps we can explore a little more. This pool, it is fabled, is bottomless and another reason for its name "Mermaid's Pool" is that it is supposed to reach the sea, and a mermaid swims along and often pops up her head to lure a poor and weary traveller into her deadly clutches. It is also fabled that when she is next seen the waters will rise up from the sea and spew out at the pool, engulfing the town of Leek which is four miles away. There is also the assertion that neither bird nor beast will drink at this pool. Indeed, so strong was the belief in the legends at one time that early in the twentieth century, around the year 1908, the Harpur Crewe family who owned the land wished to drain the pool because of the danger to sheep grazing nearby. The estate called upon its tenants to help with the work and, such was the fear that this act held for the local people that hundreds turned out on the appointed day, not just from around about but from Leek and Buxton as well. Some men did set about digging a drainage ditch, the remnants of which can still be seen to this day, but then fear engulfed them and they steadfastly refused to carry on. There were no other takers, either, despite the numbers thereabouts and so the work was cancelled. Dr Robert Plot in his work *Natural History of Staffordshire* published in 1686 said that the area around Black Mere of Morridge was "a district of noisome boggs and peat cuttings filled with stagnant water from which contagious vapours came ". He continued: "Yet are not these neither so bad as some have fancyed the water of the black-Meer of Morridge, which I take to be nothing more than such as those in the peat-pits; through it be confidently reported that no Cattle will drink of it, no bird light on it, or fly over it; all which are as false as that it is bottomless; it being found upon measure scarce four yards in the deepest place, my Horse also drinking when I was there as freely as I ever saw him at any other place, and the fowle so far from declining to fly over it, that I spake with several that had seen Geese upon it; so that I take this to be as good as the rest, notwithstanding the vulgar disrepute it lyes under."

Just to the north of the pool, and across the road, is the site of a tumulus called Merryton Low. Little can be seen of it now and an ordnance survey height marker or trig point stands close by. It was recorded in 1840 that there were stones around it although there are none now. Five minutes with the divining rods on a bitterly cold August evening, by the light of a glorious orange sky lit by the setting sun confirmed there had, in fact, been about twenty stones in a circular formation some forty feet in diameter. North, north east of Merryton Low is an area called Noonsun. This is exactly on the bearing of sunrise at the summer solstice from Merryton Low (from the true meridian and at five degrees elevation).

As we travel past the Mermaid Inn, another example of a hostelry taking the name of nearby tradition (it was undoubtedly a drover's inn and used to be called Blake Mere House) a number of upright stones will have been by the side of the road. These are in fact, there to guide the traveller in heavy snow – not, by any means, uncommon thereabouts.

Captured in time at Noon Sun Farm, Newtown, close by Longnor, in the early 1930s. Bobby the horse was owned by Len and Doris Stockton. Mr Stockton can just be seen at the reins. The young lady is Ella Ashton, their niece (my mother). They were preparing to go to Leek market one Wednesday morning.

A few hundred yards south, south east of the Mermaid is a farm and an area known as Hobhay. A "hay" is a clearing or an enclosure but it is the prefix "Hob" that attracts the interest. Close by the farm are some tumuli, burial sites of people who were alive some one thousand or so years before Christ. There is a large burial mound on Brampton East Moor near to Chatsworth House called Hob Hurst House, incidentally, and this Bronze Age round barrow derives its name from the same source as the Morridge burial site. Both sites, like several others across the British Isles, derive their name from being, it is thought, the dwelling place or the actual home of a "bogeyman" or boggart called Hob Hurst who also goes by the name of Hob Thrush and, sometimes, Hob Thrust. Boggart Hole Clough in Lancashire is from the same derivation. Jennifer Westwood in her book *Albion, A Guide to Legendary Britain* also refers to Obstrush Tumulus in North Yorkshire which in the nineteenth century was known as "Obtrush Rook" – the home of a Hobthrush. She says that the Hob may one have been a domestic spirit like a Brownie (akin to a poltergeist), whereas the Hobhurst lived in the wild. The name Brownies in the Wincle and Wildboarclough area refers to the "gentle people " or the fairy folk, by the way. Jennifer Westwood says the Hobthrush was a "frightening bogle" and Alfred Lord Tennyson wrote of it:

a jolly ghost, that shook
The Curtain, whined in lobbies, tapt at doors,
And rummaged like a rat.

Our journey south along Morridge brings us by the hamlet of Thorn-cliffe. There is a tumulus a few feet west of the road between the moor ridge and Ankers Lane. This name implies there was a hermit or anchorite living close by. It may well be this holy man, although quite possibly an anchoress (a holy woman) was in charge of the Morridge highway. This was not unusual in the days of the Norman conquerors and indeed before that period, and this ridgeway would have been extremely important both commercially and strategically over those centuries. A holy person, an anchorite who had taken vows of chastity and of isolation, would have been a good choice for the local Lord or Earl to have put in charge of the highway, collected fees and be relied upon to ensure safe passage. So reliable were these people that the first manned lighthouse, Trinity, was staffed by an anchorite. Ankers Lane leads to the moor ridgeway and there is little doubt that this name is a remnant from the days of a "road keeper" there.

Ankers Lane lead southwards to an area called Easing, which is on a small hillside. The thirteenth century charters of Dieulacresse Abbey (some two miles west of the spot) have the area as Esynge and also as Hesinge. The suffix *ing* means, in that context, "place" or piece of land, probably a pasture. It is quite possible that the prefix *Es* is the name of a god and therefore Easing is the site of a place of worship in pagan (pre-Christian) times.

Continue south and it is not far to the next very special site. This is Wormlow Farm. "Low" or "Lowe" is Anglo Saxon and means a burial mound, barrow or tumulus. "Worm" or "Wyrm" is another name for a dragon and comes from the Norse word *ormr*. Was there, therefore a dragon buried at the place? Some would say highly unlikely and others may say it is a possibility. The dragon or worm represented the force of evil and just what that force of evil may have been it is hard to envisage now, for the burial mound is as old as thirty centuries. So what might it have been? The strongest possibility is that "worm" in this context was the name given to something unChristian and so it is possibly referring to the fact that a pagan person is buried there, or that the site was venerated by the so-called heathens. A second possibility is that it is the spot of a "dragon line" or earth energy line, nowadays referred to as ley lines (see the chapter on the Nook of Fools). In extremely close proximity there is a cross, an upright monolith, standing alone in a field, easily viewed from the Moor Ridgeway. It had been said this is a parish boundary mark and may very well be used for that purpose nowadays, but it is far too tall and too elaborate and far too old to always have been a boundary marker. It does not require much deduction to conclude that the cross marks the spot of the dragon and a search with the aid of dowsing rods would soon unearth the solution.

The ridgeway can, depending on which direction the traveller wishes to take, join the main Leek to Ashbourne A523 from here to veer south east towards Waterfall and another cross site. If the crossroads on the main road are chosen then the area arrived at is Bottom House (the house at the bottom, south, of the ridgeway). The public house on these crossroads is called the Green Man and in this context is probably a reference to Puck, Robin Goodfellow, Jack in the Green or the Green Man of fertility rites (all the same chap), or a reference to the fact that this is where the travelling doctor or herbalist would pay a regular visit – the doctor's surgery of olden days. The green man referred to the greenery that the travelling healer brought with him: the herbs and vegetation that were used instead of the chemicals we use to cure us today. Wherever the sign of the Green Man hung, usually at the meeting of a number of highways, then the traveller on the packhorse trail or ridgeway would be able to call in and receive treatment, as well as the odd "medicinal" nip of alcohol as well. It is most probable that overnight accommodation would be laid on as well should the journeymen require it. Perhaps in the summertime a few pennies would be saved by sleeping under the stars but in the winter it would be money very well spent.

As we have already seen, the area round Morridge is full of hidden gems, and though we leave it to explore elsewhere, there is a little more to be seen in the area. To the east of Morridge is the expanse of land known as Butterton Moor where the River Hamps flows. Right by Morridge on Butterton Moor we come across another reference to Hob, this time at Hobmeadows, a little way down from Wormlow and the cross, sometimes referred to as High Cross. There is also a hill called Golden Hill which, like Shining Tor over at Goyt Valley, is a reference to the Otherworld. A "shining" or "golden" hill was a place where people not of this world: the fairy folk or the spirits of the ancients, would meet atop and these were the places that superstitious country folk would not traverse unless absolutely necessary.

Butterton Moor itself is famous, or infamous, as being the haunt of the headless horseman. This spectre or ghost, which may very well have its origins in the golden hill, the Otherworld, is said to ride across the moor. Many farmers in days gone by have sworn they have seen the horseman ride by and they may well have been told this story by their forefathers. Just how long it has gone on we do not know, but the headless rider (a throwback to the Celtic cult of the head) and the horse, which is usually white (again the Celtic symbolic animal) in the area awash with Hobgoblin names and places of the Otherworld, not to mention ancient burial mounds and dragon sites, could very well have been around for over a thousand years in one form or another.

In the early Spring of 1992 I spent a delightful evening with a couple of Leekensians, Mr and Mrs Pace, who has retired to a neat and cared for house in Congleton Road, Macclesfield. They had been ramblers throughout their lives and, although advancing years prevented them moving about as much as they would have liked, would retrace their favourite walks together in their memories each and every evening before retiring. They told me some delightful stories of their days spent rambling in the hills and dales around the Roaches, over Morridge and on Butterton Moor. They also told me about an infamous night of May the seventh and eighth in the year 1993 when an organised ghost hunt was held at Butterton Moor, in search of the headless horseman. In point of fact it was Mr Pace, then the secretary of Leek rambling club, who decided to get the evening going. The ramblers converged on Titterton's Farm in Dog Lane where the horseman was supposed to ride through a barn wall. In consequence it was known as the "haunted barn". Howe-ver, the "ghost hunt" has been advertised in the editorial columns of the Leek Post and there was not a mere handful of people by any stretch of the imagination. There was a great crowd, including Ralph de Tunstall Sneyd who lived just down the road at the time. Ralph, a gentleman of the old order, was a follower of the Druidic religion and we meet him in the chapter on the Manifold Valley and Thor's Cave. Oh, and of the hunt itself ... no spectre was seen, so I understand.

Assembled for the ghost hunt on Butterton Moor, 7th and 8th May 1933. The "hunters" are waiting at Titterton's Farm, Dog Lane. (L. Pace).

Old Ramshaw

In October of 1992, I had the privilege of being invited to the home of a former chairman of Leek Magistrates, Mr John Sales. Mr Sales welcomed me to his beautiful home and escorted me into his book-lined study and there we sat for hours upon hours as he related stories of the Roaches and Leek and of his 70 years as a Preacher on the Methodist Circuit. As he cut up part of a pigtail of thick black twist pipe tobacco with a silver penknife and then carefully packed it into his well used pipe he mused on my surname, Pickford, and started to recall the many members of that family he had known. They were all from the Meerbrook, Upperhulme and Roaches area and he had no problem whatsoever in deciding which of them stood out in his memory above all the others. That person was Old Ramshaw, a remarkable character whose real name was William Pickford and who received his nick name because of the area of the Roaches, Ramshaw, where he was born and bred.

Mr Sales took his mind back to 1927 when as a young man and a newly qualified Preacher he cycled up the old Roman Road from Leek to Buxton on his way to Hazelbarrow Chapel for the Sunday afternoon service, due to begin at 2 p.m. Another service usually followed at 6 p.m. This tiny chapel was built on to the side of the barn at Newstone Farm situated on the road leading down to Goldsitch Moss. This road, if that is what it could be called in those days, was nothing more than a bit of turf and a few stones. The upkeep of all these minor roads was the ultimate responsibility of the Country Surveyor for the District, Mr Angus Kinnison, whose task it was to allocate work on these roads to a number of men whose "tools of the trade" were nothing more than a hammer for the stone. They laid or re-laid stone and also turf on the roads, but some unscrupulous gentlemen would think nothing of filling in the potholes with old churns and disguising them with turf when the surveyor came to inspect. However, I am digressing somewhat although I hope it gives an indication of the rugged state of the area.

I must return to the melancholy tale of old Ramshaw as told to me by Mr Sales. Just before this young Preacher had embarked on his strenuous uphill journey to the tiny chapel on the Roaches (which boasted a congregation of about 20 seated on four small pews) he had been warned about William 'Old Ramshaw' Pickford by his father, himself a staunch and devout Methodist. "Whatever you do, don't stare at his ears" he was told. Just why this warning was given, we shall learn later.

Young John Sales cycled off the main Leek to Buxton road and along the minor road which eventually would lead to Gradbach. An even tinier and even more rugged road turned off this one to the place of worship. He parked his bicycle in the porch and walked in to the small meeting room where he first laid eyes on Old Ramshaw. Mr Sales described him as "looking like a piece of the Roaches" themselves. His craggy face was hardened by the weather, his deep dark eyes were the eyes of sorrow but also the eyes which mirrored a warm heart and showed him to be a man of good will. "He sat there in the second pew like a King surveying his land." Mr Sales remembered. "I said not a word but when to the pulpit arranged all my papers. I pulled out my pocket watch and saw it was coming up to 2 p.m. when the service should start. Just then this craggy looking gent with a noble beard spoke to me across the front pew and said 'Young man, my timepiece says two o'clock. I thanked him but did not know quite what to do because the organist (Mrs Shilkcock) had not turned up. 'Would she be coming?' I asked the small assembly. There was no reply. This gentleman – the renowned Old Ramshaw of Stake Gutter Farm – said it was time to start so I got up and gave out the first hymn. Mr Pickford pulled out a tuning fork from his waistcoat, struck it on the pew in front, scaled and pitched and found the right note and started off the hymn with a beautiful resonant voice. Out came the tuning fork again and the same procedure was followed except no-one knew this particular tune except Old Ramshaw who ploughed through it word perfect and in perfect pitch and melody. He did exactly the same with the next and the final hymn was sung with even more gusto and veracity.

"After the service I shook hands with what few people were there and then his great figure stood before me, very tall and as broad as he was long. He invited me to come to tea with him and the two of us walked up towards the turnpike road whereon lay his farm. What I noticed as we were walking up the road was that his trousers were made from two separate materials, the front of them made from cloth and the rear from corduroy. He sported a red spotted neckerchief and a big check tweed coat covered his loins."

Mr Sales caressed his much-used pipe with his hands as he continued the story. "When we reached Stake Gutter Farm we sat at the table. He fetched a loaf and cut in into good thick slices and I noticed as he went to the oven (banked up with peat) there was a teapot faintly whistling as if an angel was trying to get out. The tea was well brewed. He went to the oven and took out a large baking tin and I could smell the toasting cheese in it. It was mouth watering. He cut the cheese straight down the middle and said "Hafe for thee and hafe for may.' (half for you and half for me) and then 'Aks God's blessing on't and I'll get thay a cup a tay'.

"Tea being over he opened a drawer and I noticed some clothes lying on the top. 'Ay wuz marreet in thatn o'er fifty years agoo' he said, pointing to a suit of indigo."

"After tea we sat down on the settee, behind which was a window looking out towards Morridge. The last rays of the sun reflected on the window panes and then they disappeared. He went to the drawers again and pulled out a large tin whistle or a flageolet and sat himself down and began to play. It was magnificent. When he had concluded he dug me in the ribs with his elbow and said "What dust think o that?' It was the Sailors Hornpipe or something similar he had played and then he asked me what else I would like to hear. Handel? Mozart? Mendelssohn? and then began to play Handel's Overture from the Messiah. It was gentle and it was entrancing and it conjured up the voices and the heart of shepherdesses as they walked the hills and the dales of Ramshaw.

I asked him where he had been able to learn music of that quality and he told me he had been the conductor of Buxton Silver Prize Band for over 25 years. My eyes danced with joy to see this gentle giant with his tin whistle. A moorland musician of grace and charm."

So why had Mr Sales been warned not to stare at Old Ramshaw's ears? Well, for the answer to this tale of melancholy must be related.

In the year 1853, Tittesworth reservoir near Meerbrook was being constructed to water the needy mouths of the Potteries and a good deal of local labour was hired to barrow away the earth. Every ounce of soil had to be manhandled and young William Pickford, later to be known as Old Ramshaw, joined the workforce. He was placed in charge of a gang of Irish labourers and everything went fine until one of them asked him if he could borrow the princely sum of £3 in order that he could travel back to Ireland because, he had heard, his mother died and he wished, not unnaturally, to attend the funeral. After much deliberation and no doubt much persuasion, William Pickford agreed, providing the man signed an IOU. William got a piece of paper, no doubt very similar to the sugar bag paper on which people used to write their wills, and wrote out the IOU and, as the man could not write his signature placed his "X". Off he went and was not seen for some time so presumably he did go to Ireland and he did, indeed, return to the moorland reservoir construction site. William duly asked for the redemption of the loan and the man refused to pay him back, striking out at William who took an active stance and the fight continued for over three quarters of an hour until both of them exhausted cried "quits". William resolved to take the man to court, because £3 in those days was a considerable amount of money, especially to a young man of William's nineteen summers. The nearest civil claims court was in Macclesfield and William duly filed a claim there and attended on the appointed date. The other man did not turn up and so William told his story to the presiding judge who asked the plaintiff if he could provide proof of the claim. William produced the IOU but such was the state of the piece of paper, having been carried around in his pockets for many months, during which he had been barrowing many tons of soil and sand, that most of the words were obliterated. The judge inspected it but could make little or nothing out of the soil-stained scrap. In fact the only part of the paper that was legible was "ford", part of the name "Pickford" which influenced the judge into believing that William had brought a false claim to the court and duly sent him to prison for two months.

Never was there a young man of greater integrity and a greater martyr to honesty than William Pickford as he languished in the jail.

Having served his harsh and unjust sentence William was released and returned home, but found that among the highly religious and strict Methodist community to which he belonged by birthright, few, if any, would speak to him. He had to travel the length and breadth of the land to find work as a labourer and often had to sleep rough in a barn or under a hedge. It was, apparently, when he was forced to sleep under a hedge one night because there was no other shelter that he laid his head to rest on the grass underneath. The night developed into a bitterly frosty one of such severity that his ear became fixed to the frosty grass, and when he pulled away a portion of his ear was pulled away as well. He carried the marks and the stigma of his suffering on his left ear throughout his life.

William was obviously a hard working person because when he had gathered together enough money he returned to the area of his birth and purchased Stake Gutter Farm. In later years, I understand, he also owned two other farms at nearby Longnor.

Old Ramshaw was one of those characters still talked about with affection by local people. Everyone who knew him has a different tale to tell. Characters have abounded throughout the stretch of land we are putting under the microscope in this book. Leek, for instance in the early part of this century had characters called Baccabox, Chinkaponk, Neck-anpiff (who has such a long neck that when he turned he did it with such grace that no-one saw him move ...). Billy Buckbean and Ponka Stonier. Macclesfield had Ikey Earles, Charley from Rainow and Big Bertha among others.

Old Joe's Memories

When you are born around the highest village in England and you survive the harshest winters Mother Nature can throw at you, then you know you are of hardy stock. To have lived among some of the finest people on this planet and to have spent most of your years with your head, literally, in the clouds, is bound to linger in your memory banks. Experiences and emotions come easily in this high land around Flash and the Roaches, and it can surely be no wonder that so many legends and superstitions abound and belief in that which is not explained through the natural processes of life (the supernatural) can be brought so readily to the fore. Later we shall look at some of the weird and some of the wonderful threads that make up the magical and mystical tapestry of the land around and on the Roaches. But for the moment I would ask you to share my enjoyment of a fine character whom I first had the privilege of meeting in the late summer of 1992, and whose memory of this rich landscape all of three score years and ten ago and more were as bright and as sparkling when he related them to me as they must have been back in those days when television and radio had not been invented.

Joseph Jones, a man of the hill country, pictured at his home at Sutton, near Macclesfield, in 1992 when Joe was 92 years of age.

My first meeting with Joseph Jones was to be as result of one of those happy and intended coincidences that have been given by an eminent psychologist called Jung the description or appendage "synchronicity". A good friend of mine named Ken Whittaker, who lives at Sutton, had been calling at Joe Jones' County Council bungalow just across the road from his own house at least once a day ever since he had befriended Joe, a sprightly 93 year old with a sense of humour and a twinkle in his eyes that could, I'm sure, still attract the ladies. Ken had volunteered to chop firewood for Joe and to make sure everything was alright at his "sheltered" bungalow. When my last book (*Myths and Legends of East Cheshire and the Moorlands*) hit the bookshops Ken was one of the first to purchase a copy and one day showed it to Joe.

"This young Pickford, he's a relation of mine" said Joe to Ken after he had glanced through the contents. "I knew his grandad and his great grandad up at Flash" he said.

Ken was on the telephone to me and an arrangement was made for me to visit Joe who wanted to share all memories, happy and sad, of that area – and to see his second (or is it third) cousin for the first time.

I lost no time in driving the short distance to Sutton and Joe was waiting for me outside his spick and span bungalow. He was sitting on a wooden bench in the porch sheltering from the rain and I was chuffed to see that he had done me the great honour of putting on his obvious, best suit and a crisp white shirt for the occasion. We met shook hands and I was invited to sit alongside him on the wooden seat. Within seconds Joe's mind had returned to those days at the turn of the twentieth century when he was a young lad at a farm just outside Flash.

His mind was enormously active for his wonderful age and I sat entranced as he told me this and he told me that about the past. In fact I sat so entranced that I did not take any notes and had to return again and ask the poor old chap to go through it all again, which he did with a gusto and, I'm glad to say, he threw in a lot more titbits for good measure.

Joe's mother had died, he told me, when he was only three months old and so his grandparents Joseph Mellor and Elizabeth (known as Liza) brought him up. He married Ada Belfield from Leekfrith – one of a family of fourteen children – at Wildboarclough Church, went to work at 'Clough Mill for Lord Derby and lived thenceforth at the 'Clough. Another section of his life was taken up by the First World War when he volunteered for the North Staffs Regiment, but this was the only part of his 93 years I could not get him to speak about. "That's all best forgotten" he said. "Too many died for nowt".

While he was living at the "back of the Roaches" he knew virtually everybody. One of the major recollections of that time was the fact that the entire area was almost a township, there were so many people living there. They worked in the dozen or so coalmines which were on either the Harpur Crewe estate lands or the Brocklehurst of Swythamley Hall lands. Also, there were some pits on the land belonging to Lord Derby. "There were churches, schools, cobblers, carpenters, there was everything you could wish for in those days. There were more people living up there than in a lot of villages today" he said. He rolled his eyes and then closed his eyelids. "I'll tell you some on en" he said to me. "At ready?"

I assured him I was and away he went. "Well, the Barbers lived at Green Farm and the Goodwins at Cross Side. Brunts lived at Back o the Cross and I think Bower Brunt lived at Sutton. Joe Brunt lived at Hanging Stone Farm and his brothers Fred, George and Jim all went to live at Mayfield. Old Mother Warrington lived at Wicken Walls and her son Bill was with her, then there was the Belfields at Hawk's Nest. There were three sets of Mellors: the Mellors at Black Bank (which was pronounced Bonk) and which was below Shaw Bottom, the Mellors on Morridge and my own lot of Mellors on my grandfather's side. There was a brother at Ladmanlow, one at Newstone called Tommy I think who used to work at Top Pit coalpit above Flash. There was Jack who lived at Shaw Bottom and he was nicknamed 'Rappit' (rabbit) and then there was Moses who went to live in the Potteries."

Joe was getting well and truly into his stride now and his memory was better then ever. "I remember Big Tom Beswick" he said "He lived at Highfield, a big posh house at Flash just below the church. He owned property at Congleton and used to go there on a pony and trap to collect rent and then come back in the pitch black night without any lamp or anything.

"There was only one policeman up there in them days. He was Bobby Foster who was stationed at Flash Village. Mind you, you didn't need a bobby really, there was never anything you could call real trouble although he did kick our breeches once or twice. He covered Gradbach, Flash, Morridge, Newstone and Goldsitch Moss on foot. He didn't even have a bike."

Joe recalled one day when he was home on leave from the army and was sent to pay the rent, which was paid once a year at "back end". He told me, "A woman came to the Travellers Rest at Flash Bar tenants (of the Harpur Crewe Estates) would come with their rent money. I wasn't wearing my uniform when I walked up there and when she saw me she told me off. I should get to the recruiting office straight away and sign up for King and country she said. I didn't say a word, I just put on my army topcoat and walked away" laughed Joe. "She was embarrassed, I'll tell, you."

The three major landowners in that area, as already mentioned, were the Harpur Crewes (the Crewe and Harpur Arms at Longnor still bears witness to them), the Brocklehurst family and Lord Derby. The only time anyone saw anything of the Harpur Crewes or Lord Derby was on or after the Glorious Twelfth. The Brocklehurst family, however, were a different matter altogether. They rode the land on their fine steeds, fished the crystal clear waters and they climbed the rocky crags. And, so Joe informed me, the then young Philip Brocklehurst fought long and hard with my grandfather, Isaac Pickford on every occasion they met. For some reason, he knew not what, they were the worst of enemies yet after they had fought they were the best of friends. The surprising part is that young Isaac, or Ike as he was known, should have found himself in a lot of trouble partaking of fisticuffs with the young lord of the manor of Swythamley, but apparently Sir Philip senior encouraged these set-to's, according to Joe, because they would "make a man" of young Philip.

Both respected and also at the same time revered in those days were the various gamekeepers of the titled families. Their main task was to see that the game – hare, rabbit, partridge, pheasant, fox, quail, deer and even the occasional wildcat – remained intact, only to be chased and shot by their masters. The Harpur Crewe gamekeepers were, Joe remembers, Jack Beswick and his son Jack. Tom Usher and young Tom his nephew were the keepers for Lord Derby on his land around the Clough.

Joe later worked at the sawmills and joiners shop at Wildboarclough, owned by Lord Derby. He recalled it was driven by a water wheel and was, he said, "at the back of the church". He also brought to mind that at one time it was also a carpet factory, but when Joe worked there it was for the manufacture of doors and windows for the Crag Hall estate. There was also a blacksmith's shop on the site for the many horses. The waterwheel was replaced by "loads of big batteries" when electricity came into use.

The Crag Works at Wildboarclough where Joseph Jones worked for Lord Derby and the Estate. Now most of it has been removed but the foundations are still discernible. (Picture: D. Jackson).

Joe has returned to the area around Flash on many occasions over the years but is now saddened by what he sees. "It's all gone, everyone's gone. They're all strangers there now" he said regretfully.

But his sadness was quickly dispelled when I asked him how they coped when there was illness in the family. "Well, we had old Dr Hazelwood of Buxton" he told me. "What a man he was." Joe sat back in his seat and added, "He used to visit his patients on horseback. He wore a big jacket with all his medicines in these big pockets. He never used to open gates at the farm, he'd just jump over them with his horse. He was a big fellow, very sturdy." Joe remembered the doctor visiting his farm one day and the doctor saw him smoking a cigarette. "He snatched the fag out of my mouth and said 'get some decent bacca' meaning a pipe. He was a good doctor ..." Joe thought he had been killed in a road accident in Macclesfield. Sometimes time would not prove to be on the side of Flash people and the long journey from Buxton on horseback would be far too long, especially in poor weather. So it was on occasions like that, perhaps when a child was to be born or an accident occurred in a coal pit or on a farm that someone else was needed. And that someone often proved to be Joe's grandmother, Liza Mellor. The winters were very bad, with snow and fog seeming to last forever and Liza was often called out to tend a sick person or a woman in childbirth. Joe recalls, as a youngster, having to stand outside the farm in thick fog and blow a bugle so that people travelling to visit could get their bearings by the sound.

When it snowed they were often cut off for a very long time. Snowdrifts were very high. Each "back end" every farm would kill a pig, it was almost a ritual slaughter taking place. At Cocket Knowlthere was a room off the kitchen built into the bank side. It was very cold there and salted pork was left in that room. It would last all of the winter and the family also made their own black puddings, their own butter and their own bread. With the fowl outside supplying ready meat and eggs they, like all the other farmers never starved during those freezing cold, dark and often very isolated winters.

All around the area known as The Roaches there are abandoned farmsteads. These used to house colliers and farmers, who worked the coal mines on Goldsitch Moss and Axe Edge, the majority of which closed in the early part of the twentieth century. They all have many stories to tell, if only the stones could talk.

Joe told me of an oak tree which grew down by the River Dane, near to the last farm in Staffordshire (close to the boundaries at Three Shires) which was said to be haunted. The farm wherein this oak tree grew was called Birchen Booth and is still there. One night, Joe was walking back from Gradbach and some of his friends, who knew he would be walking there, decided to play a trick on him. They put white sheets over their heads and lay in wait by the haunted oak. Joe saw them as he was walking towards home, and so did a slight detour along one of the packhorse paths and got a clod of earth coated it in cow dung and threw it at them.

There were many places reputed to be haunted around that area. There was a farm called Ives Farm which was said to be the domain of ghouls and many folk around wore amulets to ward off the evil spirits. We shall look at these further later on but before we leave before we leave Joe, here is a final tale he told me.

"I don't know whether that oak tree was haunted or not. I never saw anything in it but I was walking near to it one night and opened a farm gate to go through. I stopped to let a dog through and then turned around. There was nothing there."

6

VALLEY OF THE MANIFOLD

I have spent many happy and idyllic hours wading in the sparkling River Manifold around Swainsley Hall in pursuit of the trout and grayling. Not, it must be said, emulating the hunter-gatherers of old, for my catches always, without fail, were returned to the swift-flowing water. Nearer to the truth would be that I was benefiting from a healing therapy beyond price but given freely by Mother Nature.

To be close to nature, in harmony with your surroundings and aware of everything that is happening around you while, at the same time, totally engrossed in your pursuit is a pastime I can vouch for; it is therapeutic and it is a delight. It was here one summer's eve as the Mayfly were darting, the dippers were collecting for their fledglings and the old grey mare in the field by the river was dreaming of its younger days that I saw, for the first time, a kingfisher. The orange rays of the lazy sun were shining like golden shafts through the trees overhanging the Manifold as the small majestic creature flew along the river's path. As each ray kissed its feathers they exploded into neon blue and those timeless moments became etched into my memory forever.

This river cannot have changed much for thousands of years and I cannot have been the first, and won't be the last, to have felt spiritually uplifted by merely being there. Neolithic hunter-gatherers would not, like I did, have returned their catches to the water goddess except for special ceremonial purposes; they would have added their catch to a meal of, maybe, bear, boar or bird. They would have taken their catch up to the hills where caves gave shelter but where wooden constructions at the entrances gave even more shelter.

Swainsley Hall is a delightful residence, also used as a place for wedding receptions and other special functions. It is ideal, and so too thought some film-makers in the 1970s who used the hall for location shots for the re-make of *The Wicked Lady*, the story of a female highway robber. It was built in 1867 by a solicitor from London, but Sir Thomas Wardle, a silk magnate and a shareholder in the Light Railway, bought it some 25 years later. He entertained a number of pre-Raphaelites here, including William Morris. Today, the town of Leek bears architectural homage to these people in a number of its fine buildings.

Byron fell in love with the River Dove, but a neighbour of this romantic river, flowing through Staffordshire, is equally romantic. Its many folds and its habit of disappearing into the limestone and surfacing further down make it unique. The Valley of the Manifold has been virtually inaccessible, save for when a tiny toy railway chugged through it for a few years, and it shows. The motor car has not overtaken its charms and if you want to get to its heart there is still really only one way, and that is to walk.

The Leek and Manifold Light Railway, for thirty years from 1904, steamed through the valley from Waterhouses to Hulme End, some eight miles. Investors were tempted by the copper mines at Ecton being re-opened and the promise of much use by the farming community but the iron horse (or pony in this case) proved to be a white elephant. The promoters of this railway mentioned in their prospectus the likelihood of Ecton Mines being used again. The Duke of Devonshire, after all (it is said) constructed the magnificent Crescent at Buxton out of his share of the profits from one single year. Some profits. When the railway closed it left a legacy rich and rare, it left the track on which the walker (and cyclist) could go with safety and with pleasure.

This river, like others we have mentioned, is born on Axe Edge, just off the Leek to Buxton road. There, some 1,700 feet above sea level it emerges from a flash (a boggy piece of land, from which the nearby village gets its name) and within its first mile and a half descends some 700 or so feet, flowing past Longnor and Brund and then, at Hulme End (where the Light Railway terminated) it enters the Manifold valley proper.

This river is infamous for disappearing underground into limestone fissures and around the years 1830 local people set about trying to block these fissures below Redhurst Cliff. The venture proved unsuccessful.

In the charming book *In the Highlands of Staffordshire* by W.H.Nithsdale (1906 and now reprinted) the river is from here described: "To my mind the Manifold's chief claim to fame lies in the fact that, from below the Wetton Mill to Ilam, it runs a double course. It lives a double life so to speak. The one, obvious: open to the heavens; making fertile the strip of adjoining meadow land, and serving as a watering for the numerous cattle and sheep, as well as affording sport to the disciples of Izaak Walton. The other hidden and subterranean, and in a dry season insidiously draining every drop of the precious water from the useful bed above; making life miserable for the farmer and his stock; surprising and driving away the unsuspecting camper-out; leaving the stepping stones high and dry and for the time being superfluous, and here and there a pool – with imprisoned trout – which eventually becomes absorbed by evaporation."

ECTON, MANIFOLD VALLEY.

The Light railway went by the side of the hill at Ecton.

There are a number of caves in this valley, caves that have been used by man and by beast, for archaeological digs, and the odd happening across by chance, have disclosed relics. One such cave (we shall come to the most famous in a little while) goes by the name of Old Hannah's Hole. It was here that seekers of archaeological treasure were digging some time in the 1800s and an explosion occurred, it is said because of electrical forces. There is a legend that thunder and lightning occurs actually inside this spot. Certainly it is often the case that a rumbling explosion can be heard within the cave when the wind is in a particular spot. The cave itself is shaped like a horn. During thunder storms people swear they have seen steam coming from fissures and people have gone on record as having witnessed a "flash and rattle" together coming from the cave. The rattle has been likened to a hug bass drum. It must be a frightening experience and just imagine how awe-inspiring this phenomenon must have been to people in the past.

The area around Wetton Mill in the Manifold Valley. Is this the setting for the Green Chapel in the Old English tale of Gawain and the Green Knight? Some would say it is, others would say the Bridestones fit the bill, and yet more say Lud Church is the site.

But not as awe-inspiring to the cave attributed to the thunder god. Thors Cave, chosen as the setting for a Gothic horror fantasy film *The Lair of the White Wyrm* by the famous Ken Russell, has been looked upon as something special for centuries.

The writer in *In the Highlands of Staffordshire* describes a journey on the Light Railway and coming across Thor's Cave for the first time: "Thor's Cave, a large cavern in the face of a bleak and forbidding majestic limestone cliff standing sentinel full four hundred feet sheer above the river, the most impressive spectacle along the whole length of this wonderful valley, played hide and seek with us as we journeyed steadily up". The writer's travelling companion's loquacity was curbed "by the stately magnificence of that gaunt, grey, black-holed headland dedicated to the Scandinavian god of thunder, as it showed itself now on our right and now on our left, while we in our pigmy train approached its base."

Gorsedd Ceremony

What a majestic spectacle this cave makes. Remnants of extinct beasts, as well as remnants of cave dwellers and even Romans have been discovered, although it must be said there is much still to be discovered there. It has been used for ceremonial purposes throughout the ages, but perhaps the most bizarre was the Druiducal Gorsedd ceremony enacted on several occasions during the 1930s.

The person behind this was a very well respected and larger than life character, self-styled Knight and Bard of the Round Table and seeker of the Holy Grail, by the name of Ralph de Tunstall Sneyd who died on Midsummer's Day, 1947, aged 85.

His pedigree has been traced, rightly or wrongly, to Alfred the Great and beyond. An obituary notice in his honour said he was a man of wide interests. In religion he was an eclectic. A devout Roman Catholic, he was also a theosophist and a sincere follower of the Russian Madame Helena Petrosky Blavatsky. A true Buddhist of the reformed Hindu church he was well versed in all the non-Christian sacred scriptures.

His family tree is said to go back to Ordgar who was an ealdorman of the Devenas (Devon and Cornwall) and was a nobleman of Wessex. Ordgar's son, Edwulf, married the daughter of Ethelred the last king of the Mercians, her mother being the daughter of Alfred the Great. Their son, Leofwine, Earl of Chester, married the daughter of Athelstan, Danish Duke of the East Angles and their sons included Leofric, Earl of Mercia. Algar the son of Leofric was the Lord of the Manor of Leek about the time of the Conquest. Amongst descendants of Algar was Randle, Earl of Chester, Lord of Leek and founder of the Abbey of Dieulacresse Abbey. Leofric's brother, Godwin, left a son, Wulfricild, who held Rushton, Grindon, and other places and from this branch of the family of Ordgar descended Richard de Sneyd and so on.

Richard de Sneyd de Tunstall served under Lord Audelegh at the Battle of Poitiers in 1356 and from then, to the time of the Henrys the family prominent in Cheshire. Richard Sneyd was Recorder of Chester in the time of Henry VIII and was M.P for the City four times. His son, William, was Sheriff of Staffordshire, grantee of Keele from Henry VIII. His son, Ralphe, built Keele Hall about 1590 – later to become Keele University; and so it goes.

Now back to Ralph de Tunstall Sneyd and Thor's Cave. A reverent Druid besides everything else, he resurrected the ancient cult in Thor's Cave, restored at his own expense the pageantry of an eisteddfod and initiated many followers into the ancient rites and instructed them in the tenets of an Absolute Divine Force of Love residing in an Imperishable Land. In his own quiet, inimitable, ways he – said his obituary – "modestly taught the unity in all cults before they declined and optimistically pointed out that the scientist of today was re-discovering the ancient theory of Relativity."

The writer of the obituary continued: "I'm afraid at the time most of us felt that his thoughts were too high-browed for us, but a few are realising that his teachings were predictions of coming events and his forecasts those of a great soul. When he took us apart he spoke seriously about the Lost Word or, as he preferred to express it, his quest for the Holy Grail."

His home was at Fairview, near Onecote, where there was an altar dedicated to King Arthur. A Piece of the Giant's Causeway lay in the garden and the barn became a chapel. Inside there were two Egyptian mummies, three big bronze Buddha, a stuffed alligator, a stuffed kangaroo and other curiosities. Ralph walled his garden during the war in order to keep any invading Germans out and in the garden there was an altar said to be used for sacrifices (of, it should be said, a harmless nature).

Ralph was a seeker of the truth and, as has been mentioned, a searcher of the Holy Grail. In Ford House, Leek, a delightful building that houses an accountancy company of repute, there hangs a picture frame. Within this there is a cutting from a 1922 newspaper and several photographs of Ralph at Winchester Abbey, proudly holding aloft a sword (the self-same sword that accompanied him atop his coffin as he was buried).

Ralph de Tunstall Sneyd

The newspaper cutting reads: "Mr Ralph de Tunstall Sneyd of Fair View Hall, near. Leek, has just (1922) visited Winchester as a representative of the Order of the Round Table of which he is a knight and which he claims to be a resuscitation of the original order founded by King Arthur. It is a mystic fraternity of poets and lovers of the beautiful which upholds religion and brotherhood, chivalry and culture. It teaches that here is an element of good in all things and that the destiny of humanity is universal peace and happiness amid experiences both novel and familiar, enabling the soul to attain higher conditions. Mr Sneyd uplifted a sword – the symbol of the Knightly chivalry – before the Round Table in the Great Hall and also presented a red rose in honour of St George."

The ceremony at Thor's Cave must have elicited some looks of bewilderment for as a picture shows, the participants wore black and white hoods and robes and travelled to the base of the cave on the Light Railway.

Where the traveller on the Leek and Manifold Light Railway could get refreshments – the Light Railway Hotel at Hulme End, today still a celebrated hostelry but with a change of name.

Sir Gawain Again

Before we turn our back on the Valley of the Manifold for now and journey onwards across the Staffordshire border into Derbyshire, we must pause awhile and look at yet another contender for the Green Chapel of Sir Gawain and the Green Knight. We have already examined the hot favourite, Lud Church, in this and my previous book but now is the time to look at one in the Manifold Valley.

John Matthews has produced a thought-provoking book *Gawain: Knight of the Goddess* and journeys into our valley in an appendix to his work entitled *The Chapel in the Green*. He seeks to identify the Green Chapel and mentions that in 1948 Bertram Cosgrave in the journal *Antiquity* sites the Chapel as the Bridestones on Bosley Cloud. He adds that in the introduction to the 1940 Early English Text Society edition of Gawain and the Green Knight Miss Mable Day suggested a cave in the Manifold Valley, near Wetton Mill fitted the bill. Miss Day points out that local tradition calls this cave "Thurshole" (not Thor's Cave) meaning, she says "Fiend's house" and Mr Matthews suggests that his is a reference to the Thunder God, comparing him with the Green Knight, this site is appropriate.

Miss Day's article said: "If Sir Gawain, approaching as he would from the West, came down from Butterton Moor by the Hoo Brook, he would see (the cave) on the left side beside the weir when he reached the bottom of the valley. The bank on which the Green Knight stood would be the cliff just below the Hoo Brook, on the opposite side of the Manifold to the Green Chapel. From the top of this cliff a passage (mentioned by Plot in the Natural History of Staffordshire) and still traversable, communicates with a cave at the foot ... Issuing from thence, the Green Knight crossed the Manifold to the level ground in front of the mill, where the Beheading Game took place."

So there we have it: is the Green Chapel at the Bridestones, at Lud Church or at a cave near Wetton Mill? Certainly within the area from Alderley Edge in the west across to the Manifold Valley there is much folk lore concerning the legendary Arthur and his Knights. I am sure that Ralph de Tuntall Sneyd, who styled himself Teliesin Peredur Amadis, Knight and Bard of the Round Table, would have had something to add to this discussion.

Of the Manifold he wrote, and presumably of Thor's Cave on high:

Once the baleful fire was gleaming,
In that cavern far high
In yon mighty rock, and caldrons
For the awful gods stood nigh;
Once the crimson blood was streaming;
And the paean rose on high.

Thor's Cave: a photograph taken early this century

7

MAGIC OF THE MOORS

The dales and plains of picturesque Cheshire and the ferocious higher landscape of Northernmost Staffordshire must now, in the main, be left behind as we travel eastward in the tracks of the Irish Brigantes who traversed this way in days departed.

Limestone and gritstone mingle on the moors where barrows, cairns, henges and circles are as common as the curlew and the kestrel. It is now hard to comprehend that this land was once a huge forest wherein man, and woman and child built edifices to their departed; where their Shamans caused temples for worship to be constructed and where healing sanctuaries were developed as we today, the civilised ones, have cemeteries, churches and hospitals.

The Derbyshire Peak, stretching across to the borders of Nottinghamshire and Yorkshire, was, and still is, the land of the Green Man – Hob, Robin Goodfellow, Puck, Robin Hood or Bucca. Whatever the name it is the same creature, nature's spirit who as the outcast Robin Hood became a legendary wolfsbane, or outlaw and as the impish Puck found its way into romances and legends – the fairy tales. The super-natural being living outside the boundaries of civilisation, is still living in the hearts of people of the Peak and can still be seen in that which has been left behind. Its name is kept alive in the most famous of its tourist towns, Buxton, as we shall discover.

Today, the most venerated site left behind by the ancients within the area we shall explore is Arbor Low (or Lowe); a site, some say, as important as Stonehenge although, in fact, this awesome structure is but one of the few remaining magical and mystical sites. Time was when there would have been many similar healing and meeting places (as Arbor Low so surely is) throughout this land I am calling The Peak, not the Peak District and not the White or Dark Park but the high ground around Buxton and across to Bakewell. These places, like Arbor Low, were here, there and everywhere throughout this country we know as the United Kingdom but, over the centuries, churches have been built on the land where they stood; they have been demolished; they have been ploughed over; they have been lost forever and ever. What we see now as the Ancient Monument called Arbor Low is one of the last of many. There were larger temples in the area, that is for sure and, equally, there were many smaller ones. To say, however, that this "Stonehenge of the North" is the be all and end all of our ancient circles or henges is to obscure the obvious.

Let us just look around the outskirts of The Peak for starters. At Leek, a township famed for its friendly folk, there stands a church dedicated to St Edward the Confessor but, before the public relations machines of the day got going for this unpopular monarch, it was dedicated to St Edward the Martyr. This edifice is built atop a sandstone escarpment where there was (even as far as the official history of the Church is concerned, and that is unusual) a large stone circle. This could have been as big, if not bigger, than Arbor Low and was a site where the double sunset (investigated in my previous book) could be witnessed. From the side of the elevated ground on which it stood there flowed a small stream or brook and this, it must be presumed, would have been looked upon as special, spiritual, water. The town of Leek derives its name from this for "Leek" has developed from "Lec" meaning stream or brook. It must have been special for such a tiny outflow of water to give name to a township. Most towns have a river running through. Leek has a river, the Churnet, running round it.

Another site on the fringes of this area is Oak Grove near to Macclesfield where, until the mid 1980s there stood a henge of fine proportions.

Close by Buxton there is the equally large stone circle called The Bull Ring, a site that retained its identity by the skin of its proverbial teeth. This and the Arbor Low circle together with Wet Withers circle on Eyam Moor form the three corners of a perfect triangle. Just take a look on the Peak District Tourist Map, it's spot on. There is a certain amount of evidence that Buxton once sported a large stone circle or henge as well as housing the temple to the water goddess. Perhaps they were one in the same.

It was the Neolithic or New Stone Age people who must shoulder the blame for clearing most of the ancient forest previously flourishing around here. These people came to the area of Derbyshire around 3,000 BC and set about cultivating and clearing the land with a vengeance; so the bleakness now so much a part of the magic of the Peak we experience today was thus formed. The Celtic peoples who followed much later left their marks on the culture, beliefs and landscape as well and many traces of these folk still remain. Their magic still exists for some in the holy wells and their memories linger in the stones, in the land and in the minds. The Romans utilised existing thoroughfares and improved on them but these trackways had been around not just for trade – they had been passages between special sites. These became military roads and later were used as packhorse trails and many became turnpikes. And, as the Romans departed and the Saxons appeared, submitting to the Danes and the Normans, the spirit of Hob of the Hurst watched over the goings on. Today his legend remains as the Hooded Man in Lincoln Green whose domain is now said to have been away to the east at Sherwood. But Robin, according to the ballads, roamed the hunting grounds of Macclesfield and the hunting grounds of the Peak. As Hob he was in the wild wood at Hob Hurst House, a round barrow near Baslow and he was above the wild rocks of The Roaches where his name is also alive at a long-ago place. Just as Robin of the Hood would do, this Puckish spirit would help those in need and play havoc with the lives of those who did not need help.

Robin was likened in the ballads of the minstrels to the Earl of Chester whose heart was buried at a hunting lodge in a royal forest known as the Forest of Macclesfield and tales also tell of this Robin coming from the lands of Loxley, a village akin to Uttoxeter and close by Derby. Yes, he is still around. To the church he is the devil, says Shirley Toulson in her special book *Derbyshire, Exploring the Ancient Tracks* and she says that as the church banned Robin Hood from mass, it so used the people's belief in his "own diabolical existence" to enforce its own authority. Shirley says in her very readable and informative book that she feels Hob and companions (including the fairy folk) were real. They were pre-Celts, outcasts living, as Robin Hood, on the fringe of society and, in all probably, were used as slaves.

The television dramatisation *Robin of Sherwood* made allusions to the Green Man or Hern the Hunter ... Hen Cloud on the southern Pennine chain may well be named from Hern ... who is another example of Puck or Hob.

But let us put the man in green to one side for a while, for there are so many more riches within this land. There is so much already documented but, as I hope I have perhaps already shown, there is so much more staring us directly in the face; still here but overlooked, cast aside or discarded. This land contains so many sites of importance to the seekers of treasure and truth that another volume will blossom, I hope, in the future.

Buxton's London Road. No motor cars at the time this photo was taken, only a horse and cart in the background. Picture courtesy Buxton Advertiser.

The Peak we are looking at is a natural progression from the area of the Roaches known as Axe Edge where close by the rivers called Dove, Goyt, Manifold and Dane are all born. They share the same womb of mother earth and from this we traverse the land eastwards as far as the township of Ashbourne (where, dare I say it, there is an inn dedicated to the Green Man). The Peak derives its name not from the pointed top to a mountain but from the Pecsaetans, meaning hill dwellers, who lived in the northernmost part of the land known as Mercia around the seventh century. Both Staffordshire and Cheshire were within this Kingdom as well, and this is the domain, the land of the three shires, we are looking to. Hill forts like the one on the Shrivering Mountain, Mam Tor, and over a dozen more were there to protect a boundary before Mercia existed, but from whom we cannot now tell.

Today this land is visited by many thousands, and deservedly so. It is not an area that shrugs off the visitor, it is one that welcomes the traveller whether the journey has been short or long; a relic of the days of the jaggers whose long trains of mules and horses, bells tinkling around their necks, walked the many miles across this land of magic. The scenery is as fine as that in Scotland, its people are as welcoming; its air is bracing and its waters possess a rare healing quality. So does the land. Just stand and stare and see what I mean.

These people participating in Fairfield Cycle Parade, Buxton, 1912, would have been unawares of the true significance of the maypole, a fertility symbol. Fairfield, although geographically now part of Buxton, still looks upon itself as different to the town of Buxton. Picture courtesy Buxton Advertiser.

Stones of the Sacred Waters

It was the Romans who have been credited with establishing a fort and later a civilian settlement at Buxton, but these Legionaries were not the first to have found the area and its waters something rather special.

Today, the popular tourist centre with excellent shops and a fine theatre – the Opera House, worthy of the West End of London – attracts countless thousands. Centuries ago it did just the same but for different reasons. There were no shops then nor theatres but, no doubt, a performance could be witnessed whenever a sacred and profound ceremony was enacted.

For this area we now know as Buxton was a Grove within an ancient woodland and within this Grove there was a temple wherein the Celtic goddess Arnemetiae was worshipped and adored. The special water that flowed from within this was blessed by the water goddess and it contained magical healing qualities. Just as today, the holy well at Holywell in North Wales is surrounded by a temple, a church, and is visited by many pilgrims each year, so was this holy site at Buxton the scene of pilgrimages and the site of a temple. It was thus when the Romans arrived and it continued to be thus until the site was deliberately destroyed some four hundred or so years ago.

Woodland was the natural vegetation of this land when the seas receded and during the period known as Neolithic the peakland was a mass of trees, primarily hazel, ash and oak. The denuded state today is a result of clearance and over-farming that has gone on for countless centuries. When the Romans arrived they found the area dominated by the tribe known as Brigantes, the people of Brigit the fertility goddess. The Bridestone on Bosley Cloud was one of the earliest peak henges to be constructed by these people who came from the west, most probably Ireland and gradually worked their way eastward to the Derbyshire hills and dales and beyond.

The Romans had a fort at nearby Brough and called it Navio or Anavia and colonised the area of the Sacred Grove, giving it the name Aquae Arnemetiae, the waters of the goddess. The warm springs, maintaining a constant temperature of 82 degrees Fahrenheit, were special to those before the Romans and the pre-Christians legions were also in awe. They used it as a leave centre for troops in the region. Two Roman baths excavated in the seventeenth and eighteenth centuries were destroyed and there is evidence that the well was venerated by followers of the pagan thoughts throughout the stranglehold of Christianity. The Celtic goddess became Christianised as St Anne long after the Romans had discovered both Buxton and Christianity.

St Anne has many wells dedicated to her but she seems only to have found favour from the Middle Ages. There is a line of thought that says she was the mother of the Virgin Mary. There was, until the sixteenth century, a statue at the shrine of the water goddess and no doubt ardent Christians assumed it to be St Anne. But this statue was there when the Romans arrived and was undoubtedly the graven image of the Celtic goddess. Throughout the centuries up until the time it was removed, offerings were made to this statue and were left decked around the shrine. This angered the fervent people of the sixteenth century who took it upon themselves to reform the ways of worship in Britain and the shrine, probably over two thousand years old at that time and the statue, perhaps even older, both survived no more, at least physically. The man responsible was Sir William Bassett who destroyed the statue and shrine in 1538. Bassett wrote to Thomas Cromwell and pointed out that the well was used for healing purposes right up until the bitter end. He wrote: "According to my bounden duty and the tenor of your Lordship's letters lately to me directed, I have sent your Lordship by this bearer, my brother Francis Bassett, the images of St Anne of Buckston and St Andrew of Burton upon Trent, which images I did take from the places where they did stand, and brought them to my house within 48 hours after the contemplation of your said Lordship's letters, in as sober a manner as my little and rude wit would serve me. And for that there should be no more idolatry and superstition there used, I did not only deface the tabernacles and places where they did stand, but also did take away crutches, shirts and shifts, with was offered, being things that did allure and entice the ignorant people to the said offering."

This destroyer of history added in his letter that he had locked up and sealed the baths and wells of Buckston. (*Letters Relating to the Suppression of Monasteries*, Camden Society, 1843). However, according to Christina Hole in her book *Saints in Folklore*, before the end of that century St Anne's Well and other healing springs nearby were being visited by the sick once more though not, she writes, for religious reasons. The Earl of Shewbury built a new bathhouse in 1572 and Buxton became a spa town, with many hotels and inns springing up (forgive the pun) around the healing wells and springs. The ancient ceremonies of blessing the wells and adorning them with offerings was resurrected in the middle of the nineteenth century; proof indeed that memories had been handed down over the centuries. They were not, I would think, committed on to paper and like the tales passed on by the storytellers of old, the actions of blessing the waters were handed down. In the times around the reign of Henry VIII flowers, green twigs and garlands of holly and other evergreens were draped across the well mouths, but the Victorian revivals relied more on pretty pictures being produced by flower petals. Even so what was no doubt looked upon as a "quaint" custom to the Victorians had its roots in the pre-Roman traditions of the area. This revival of well dressing as it became ran rife throughout Derbyshire and parts of Staffordshire and, perhaps surprisingly, into certain bits of Cheshire as well. A number of these have now faded thanks to two world wars and civilisation catching up on the world but in Derbyshire they are now an added boost to the tourist industry as well as being a tradition that is being retained for whatever other reasons, most especially by the church. Just one more of many examples of the Christianisation of pagan ceremonies.

The tourist town of Buxton used to be known by the Saxons as Buckstans, Bawkestanes or Badestanes and later as Buckstones or Buckston. So here we now have the appendage "ton" meaning stone or stones. Here we have an allusion to there having been special stones within the places, most probably the stones constituting the shrine within the grove. It has also been said it could refer to stone baths but this is not very probable I feel. No, the stones were something special and they were there to mark a special spot but, alas, it must now only be conjecture as to what their actual shapes and sizes were. When Sir Joseph Paxton designed the Pavilion Gardens alongside the Opera House he placed two standing stones there. It has been said they were witness to the fascination at the time for "The Druids". I think that at that time there was still a tradition of the Buck Stones of the Grove and these two stones echo those memories. Whether they are some of the originals or merely copies it is impossible to say. There is a certain energy coming from them, but they have undoubtedly been removed to that place in the gardens and as they are not, therefore, in situ the evidence is insufficient.

But why was the town named after the Stones and who or what gave their name to them?

Here, oh surprise upon surprise, I have a suggestion to make. I feel it is not beyond the realms of possibility that here we have purely and simply another example of the earth spirit or the green man. Bucca was, and still is, the name given to an impish spirit who inhabited, and still inhabits, stones. He is related very closely to Puck, the impish spirit, who became Robin Goodfellow and thence Robin of the Hood. The stones that gave their name to our lovely town of Buxton were so called because they possessed (or formed part of) a spirit, an energy – a force that helped the common people, especially within the realms of healing waters, take from those who possessed the richness of knowledge of health and give to the poor and the sickly. My allusions to Robin Hood I must admit; but those roots from within the earth do feed the same tree.

Higher Buxton as it used to be. Courtesy Buxton Advertiser.

8

TEMPLE OF THE HEATHENS

A heathen temple, one of the most striking monuments of antiquity that is to be met with in Derbyshire, and almost in this country. With those words, Dr J. D. Sainter commenced his treatise on Arbor Low in 1878 in his work we have referred to before: *Scientific Rambles*. It is interesting, today, to see how this monument was viewed in Victorian times, and Dr Sainter gives us a ready insight in his book. He was not the first and he is not going to be the last to be fascinated by this "heathen temple" as he called it. Some say it is on a par with Stonehenge and some say it ranks in importance above Stonehenge. Others are convinced it is the kingpin of the leys of Great Britain, a major part of a mammoth zodiac, a key to Atlantis and the centre of UFO activity.

So what exactly is Arbor Low, or is it "Lowe"? It lies about nine miles south east of Buxton on the Ashbourne road and its name derives, in all probability, from *Arbhar* a Celtic name for a locality or institution suitably adapted for an assemblage of people, either for civil, military or religious purposes, and *Lowe* (Anglo Saxon or old English *hlaw*) a burial mound, barrow or tumulus, and referring to a high place. Dr Sainter drove by means of pony and trap across the moorlands to this site in 1873 and then he said this ancient relic consists of a circular (though somewhat elliptical) area or platform that will measure from east to west about 50 yards across it. It is accompanied by a ditch fifteen feet broad at the bottom; and up to a level with the area, it is about 18 feet in breadth. During its excavation, the earth was used in the construction of an outer vallum or rampart from 18 to 24 feet in height and 810 feet in circumference at the top. To the north and the south there is a path 12 yards in width that leads across the ditch on to the platform; and on the east side of the southern entrance there are the remains of a barrow that was opened in 1845 by Mr Thomas Bateman, the contents of which proved beyond doubt the extremely remote age of this burial. In addition to the earthworks, there is to be noticed a circle of stones about 30 in number, that have been prostrated, and most of them lie close to the inner margin of the ditch, along with, here and there, the remains of others that have been mutilated, displaced or broken up. The uninjured specimens consist of rough and unhewn slabs of limestone, very much weathered, and ranging from five to eight or ten feet in length, three or four in breadth at the widest part, one in thickness, and they generally point with their narrower ends towards the centre of the circle, where there are likewise some larger and thicker stones that have evidently formed part of a dolmen.

An evocative and fanciful drawing of Arbor Low by the Victorian Dr Sainter.

The site of Arbor Low is not quite so elevated as some districts in the county, yet it commands a most extensive prospect, and the feeling on visiting the places (said Dr Sainter) upon a fine summer's day when there are no sounds to disturb the solitude except the singing of the lark, and now and then the cry of the plover (which here abound), are most pleasing; still this is accompanied by a certain amount of reverential awe and amazement, especially on a first visit, when contemplating this hoary ruin along with its eventful history.

Dr Sainter was obviously quite taken with the site, and I believe he saw a lot more there than he cared to put on to paper in those strict Victorian days. However, he did hint at one or two things and I can do no better than refer to his writings once more.

He continued: The temples of the primaeval Britons are invariably circular and constructed of large masses of unhewn stone enclosed by a vallum of earth. Some few of them exist in other parts of England but none are more perfect than the circle of Arbor Lowe. Clusters of tumuli are frequently found near to these temples, raised, doubtless, under the influence of the same feelings which prompt us at the present day to inter our dead in consecrated ground. There is every reason to believe that amongst the earlier Britons the sun was the principal, if not the only embodiment of Deity generally worshipped. These circles were unquestionably the scenes of their civil meetings as well as of their religious ceremonies. The priests, it is universally known, were called Druids; they have, previous to Caesar's invasion, obscured their once simple religion with a mass of dire superstitions, and monopolised most of the power of government. About 50 yards from the south entrance to the right, there is barely visible the outline of a small barrow which has been explored ... and at a distance of about a quarter of a mile west of Arbor Lowe there is observable a large tumulus called Gib Hill which was opened by the late Mr T. Bateman in 1848. A stone chest was disclosed containing an urn, and likewise some other ancient relics, as well of those of a more modern date. The mound is connected in a serpentine form with Arbor Lowe by a small embankment of earth; and short lengths of it are here and there noticeable commencing a little to the left of the southern entrance, and outside the great rampart.

So there we have a Victorian view of the "heathen temple". In those times, as we have seen before, anything pre-Roman was attributed to the Druids, hence his references to them. We are now of a mind, of course, that the monument pre-dates the Druids by a good few hundred years, even a thousand or so. And to clear up a few facts: there are nearly 50 stones and parts of stones belonging to a circle of approximately 150 feet. To date there is very little evidence of holes underneath or by these stones where they could have stood up in but this does not preclude them having been upright; they may have been wedged upright. A skeleton has been found.

This site is a site of paradox. It is set on high, but cannot be seen. Its stones, now lying forlornly on the ground, would have been hidden had they been upright because of the mound around them and, although in line with the solstices and therefore used as a solar and lunar observatory, it is painfully obvious this was not the prime function. Ever since we have discovered that stone "circles" were aligned with the sun's phases, it has been easy to assume that because of this they were purely and simply observatories to mark the seasonal changes for farming and ceremonial purposes. But, it must be said, there would have been an inordinate waste of manpower and earth power to construct these sites, often within a couple of miles of one another, to merely show the phases of the sun and the moon. Would not, after all, one such site have been sufficient? Certainly in the case of Arbor Low there is far more evidence to support a theory that it was something much more than merely an observatory.

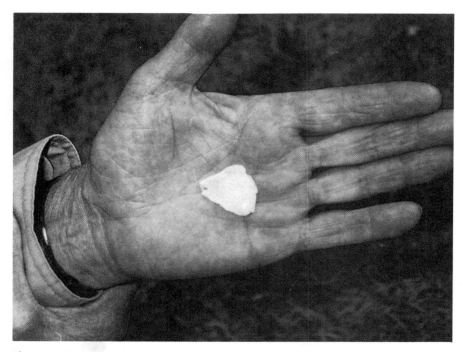

If any proof was needed that hunter-gatherers frequented the area around Arbor Low this is it. A mole unearthed this flint arrowhead onto its hill and so it was discovered less than a mile from the "Temple of the Heathens."

It probably dates from anything up to 2,000 BC and the clues lie in the ditch and mound surrounding the stones. The mound appears to have been constructed to shelter and to obscure whatever was inside. And it also appears to have been constructed as a "grandstand" so that people could witness what was going on inside, rather like the Roman amphitheatres but not graced with terraces.

So what did go on inside? Now the going gets tougher because there are not many clues. But there are some, and the biggest of the lot was a few hundred yards away close by the farm where the visitor has to deposit cash in order to journey to the site.

Park your car at the signposted car park and stroll through the farm yard, over the stile and turn left, where the path takes you alongside a drystone wall towards the Low. Nestling beneath this limestone drystone wall there was a stone of the same proportions as those resting within the circle. Only this one is different and rather special for it has a perfectly shaped circle carved in it. A healing circle. There are many examples of stones at ancient sites used for healing purposes and the vast majority have a hole through them, some big enough to enable a person to pass through and some just big enough for a limb. This one could easily take an arm or a leg and perhaps a baby's head. It is, without doubt, part of the monument and it is, without doubt, man-made.

It has been said that countless ley lines run through Arbor Lowe but I must admit that my divining rods could not pick up a vast amount of them. There is certainly a very strong one, and this has been referred to by Paul Devereux and Ian Thomson in their excellent book *The Ley Hunter's Companion*, a treatise I can heartily recommend. They paid a visit to this site and could find only two that satisfied them, one which concluded at St Bertram's Well at Illam. Bertram or Bertelin was the son of a king of Mercia who became an anchorite and who, it is recorded, performed miracles of healing at the site. An earth energy line, therefore, with the start and the finish as healing centres must have been pretty strong. In fact, it still is. There have been attempts over the centuries to mutilate this healing temple; most obviously by pushing down the stones that were placed in the ground rather like acupuncture needles but in this case to harness the natural energy the earth gives out.

I have known people who have felt the desire to sleep overnight at the Low. They have not been able to explain to me why they have needed to do so but they have said they felt the better for it. They have merely been doing what comes naturally.

During a visit to this temple of healing a few years ago, a psychic "saw" carts, pulled by horses, and loaded with people covered with animal skins. She at first thought they were bodies and had been brought for burial, but then realised they were sick people being carted to the site for one reason: to be healed. We now take afflicted people by the coach load to that miraculous and holy place in France called Lourdes; we are doing the same today as our forefathers did but at a different spot.

This place is still special. It is no longer as powerful as it used to be thanks to deliberate attempts to destroy what was there, but it can still be what you wish it to be. Just give it the opportunity.

But as I have already mentioned, this was not the only such place in the area; just as we do not have just one hospital to deal with the entire area today. There were others; some have been destroyed and lost forever and some, like The Bull Ring (SK 078783) near Dove Holes have been mutilated but still hang on for dear life. The Bull Ring would have been very similar in construction and in size to Arbor Low; it even had an embankment around it at one time, in exactly the same manner as Arbor Low. A smaller one, Wet Withins (SK 226790) on Eyam Moor is a mere baby at 95 feet in diameter with sixteen upright stones but it is remarkable in that it forms one of the three points of a perfect triangle, the other two being the Bull Ring and Arbor Low. No mere coincidence, I am certain.

The area is rich in remains of Neolithic and Bronze Age sites; thanks in no small way to the fact that we have not built over them or demolished them completely in fits of religious fervour. Stanton Moor (SK 247634), for instance, is one complete burial site with over 70 cairns, stone circles and a standing stone. It is one huge cemetery stretching across 150 acres and is unique in Great Britain, but unfortunately we do not appreciate its vast significance, I fear. It was used during the period 2,200 to 1,400 BC and goodness only knows how many people have been buried there. We do know, if we are to be logical, that it was undoubtedly a site of great importance to the people of the day for they used it just the same as we use hallowed or sanctified ground today. Nothing really changes.

There are far too many sites to mention individually but I would beg you to pay a visit to this area. There are plenty of well signposted footpaths and walk-ways and the ground is not too demanding but it is still possible to get a feeling of the spirit of the place, a feeling our ancestors knew only too well.

Stones at Arbor Low ... pushed down centuries ago to destroy what memories the earth had for them.

Undoubtedly the most famous of the sites on Stanton Moor is the Nine Ladies Stone Circle along with an upright stone to the south west known as the King's Stone or Stump. The stones here are little more than three feet in height within a diameter of some thirty three feet. There is a barely noticeable bank surrounding it and a slight mound in the centre which I am certain contained another stone at one time. The small single stone could well have been a sighting point for the summer solstice.

As with similar sites throughout the land there is a tradition that the stones were young ladies who were turned to stone for dancing on the Sabbath, an obvious attempt by puritans to ensure their ways were followed for fear of dire consequences. The ringleader of this act of defiance of the Sabbath day was said to be a fiddler, or perhaps drummer or even piper, who was also turned to rock. Jennifer West-wood in her wonderful *A Guide to Legendary Britain* feels the name Nine Ladies is not all that old. She says the word "nine" often bears little relation to the number but is a "convention" and gives a number of examples. She says it has been surmised the name "nine" in the case of another Nine Stones should actually be "none", the ninth hour of the day when the service of "Nones" was performed. The Service of Nones was moved to mid-day and it is from this we get noon.

Take the footpath from the farm yard towards Arbor Low and there, underneath a drystone wall, lay this stone; obviously once part of the "temple of the heathens" it was surely a healing stone. The hole is man-made. Returning in August, 1993, I discovered this stone had been removed.

Andrew Collins, undoubtedly one of this country's foremost researchers into the occult, went to the Nine Ladies stone circle in 1982. He and others intended to conduct a seasonal ritual meditation on the time and date corresponding with the Celtic Samhain cross quarter day. He tells of a ferocious wind that engulfed the inside of the circle at the moment the group discharged the site's energies. (*The Circlemakers*, 1992).

Andrew has done much research not only in Derbyshire but in other areas mentioned in this book, not least Lud Church and the Roaches, and I am proud to say I was able to assist him in a very small way.

The last time Hilary and I paid a visit to the Nine Ladies there had been markings made close by the King's Stone, markings that show that even today it is necessary to ensure the ways of the old are suppressed. Some idiots had obviously been playing at their own form of black magic nearby and this may have prompted some well meaning person to make the sign, in runic letters, "Christos", or Jesus Christ, Or it may have been because of the old ways which used to be followed and perhaps still are that it was felt necessary to sanctify the site.

Derbyshire has an elegance of ancient sites, far too many too explore in this chapter but, as I have already hinted, perhaps one day we shall look at the area in greater detail and I hope you will be able to join me on this journey when it is undertaken.

Until that time, please go out and about in this wonderful Shire; it is geared to the day tripper, the motorist in search of something special and the hiker plodding its paths. It is no hardship to spend a while here. Wherever you go there is evidence of the past, for few Counties in the entire kingdom can match its riches.

9

DIVISIONS OF THE YEAR

As the Earth revolved around the Sun or, as it was thought by most, the Sun traversed the heavens, there were times when its journeys changed course and changed the climate, making the days longer or shorter, bringing the great winds and the rain or heralding the season of little water. People say the Great Stones were erected to chart the course of the Sun. Maybe, but did they need to refer to the Great Stones year after year? Perhaps the Stones did indeed chart the travels of the Sun and perhaps they also took from the Sun and from the Earth and gave to Man. Fires needed to be lit to help the Sun stay in the sky and to cleanse the beast, and a watch needed to be kept for the wild spirits that roamed on certain nights. These were the major seasonal festivals:

MIDWINTER SOLSTICE (21st December)

At which fire ceremonies were held to help the re-birth of the Sun and to ensure its return. Later it became Christ's Mass or Yuletide. The midwinter revels are not of Celtic roots but Scandinavian and Saxon, celebrating the life-force dormant but waiting to emerge. In the fourth century the Church designated 25th December as Christ's birth date.

CANDLEMASS (1st February)

Festival named by the Celts *Oimelc* or *Imbolc* to celebrate the re-birth of the mother goddess (Earth) and the start of Spring. An important Celtic Quarter Day Christianised as Candlemass.

SPRING EQUINOX (end of the third week of March)

The Saxons held the festival of the goddess *Eostre* around this date and it was adopted by the Church in the fourth century to commemorate and celebrate the resurrection of Christ. Eostre's familiar or totem creature was a hare who gave a gift of an egg, the symbol of new life. The hare has become the Easter Bunny.

MAY DAY (1st May)

Beltaine or *Bealtain* to the Celts. The start of summer and the time of Walpurgis Night; the day and night for planting the first crops when the Earth is at its most fertile when the Maypole, a fertility symbol, was danced around. It has been taken under the wing of the Church as Rogationtide. The god *Belenos* or *Baal* could aid the health of livestock at this time.

MIDSUMMER SOLSTICE (21st June)

The longest day and the Feast of Sol the Sun god, celebrated by the lighting of fires. The entire countryside would, in the past, have been ablaze with great fires lit upon the sacred high points. People would jump through the flames and livestock were sent through the flames as a cleansing and promotion of good health. Later the ashes were scattered on fields as a fertility aid.

LAMMAS (1st August)

The Feast of Lughnasad which became *Lammas* (Anglo Saxon) a time of celebration. It came the celebration of the start of the harvest in Christian times. It was named after Lugh the Shining One who killed Balor of the Baleful Eye.

AUTUMN EQUINOX

First week of September. Still celebrated at Abbots Bromley in Staffordshire by the Horn Dance, a fertility rite most probably connected with the Celtic horned god.

MARTINMASS (1st November)

Samhain of the Celts, a festival of fire to defend against the trails of the forthcoming weather and a fear of losing the Sun. The time of Halloween, All Hallows Eve. Samhain marked the beginning of the year when the Earth opened and spirits escaped to travel abroad. The Night of All Souls.

BIBLIOGRAPHY

Ball, Harry, *Place Names in the Moorlands*, 1991 (Leek Historical Society).

Billington, Sandra, *A Social History of the Fool*, Harvester Press Ltd, 1948.

Bord, Janet & Colin, *Sacred Waters*, Granada Publishing, 1985.

Branston, Brian, *Lost Gods of England*, Book Club Associates, Thames & Hudson, 1974.

O'Brien, Chirstian, *The Megalithic Odyssey*, Turnstone Press, 1983.

Briggs, Katharine M., *The Vanishing People*, B. T. Botsford Ltd., 1978.

Brocklehurst, Sir P., *Swythamley & Its Neighbourhood*, 1874.

Burland, C. A., *Echoes of Magic*, Peter Davies, London, 1972.

Cattegno, Jean, *Lewis Carroll, Fragments of a Looking Glass.*

Christian, Roy, *The Peak District*, David & Charles, 1976.

Collins, Andrew, *The Circlemakers*, ABC Books, 1992.

Cooper, J. C., *An Illustrated Encyclopaedia of Traditional Symbols*, Thames & Hudson, 1978.

Davies, C. S., *A History of Macclesfield*, The University Press, 1961.

Dawson, Cyril H., *Langley, the History of a Cheshire Village*, Langley Centre, 1989.

Devereux, Paul and Thomson, Ian, *The Ley Hunter's Companion*, Thames & Hudson, 1979.

Earwaker, I.P., *East Cheshire*, 1877.

Field, John, *English Field Names*, David & Charles, 1972.

Hole, Christina, *Saints in Folklore*, G. Bell & Sons 1966.

Hudson, Derek, *Lewis Carroll, An Illustrated Biography*, Constable & Co., 1954.

Laughton, Jane, *Seventeenth Century Rainow*, Heathland Printers, 1990.

Matthews, John, *Gawain: Knight of the Goddess*, Aquarian/Thorsons.

Nithsdale, W. H.,*In the Highlands of Staffordshire*, Moorlands Press, 1906 (reprint Churnet Valley Books, 1992).

Transactions of the North Staffs Field Club, 1920 – 28.

Ormerod, George, *The History of the Country Palatine of Cheshire*, 1819.

Pepper, Elizabeth & Wilcock, John, *Magical and Mythical Sites*, Weidenfield & Nicolson, 1977.

Rathbone, Clifford, *Dane Valley Story*, Macclesfield Press Ltd., 1974.

Rathbone, Clifford, *Goyt Valley Story*, Macclesfield Press, 1969.

Renaud, M.D., Dr Frank, *Ancient Parish of Prestbury*.

Richards, Raymond, *Old Cheshire Churches*, B. T. Batsford, 1947.

Rowley, Gordon, M. A. (Cantab), *Macclesfield in Prehistory*, 1978.

Sainter, J. D., *Scientific Rambles around Macclesfield*, Swinnerton and Brown, 1878).

Senior, Michael, *Myths of Britain*, Orbis Publishing 1979.

Smith, Walter, *Over The Hills*, Courier Office, 1921.

Smith, Walter, *Forest & Clough*, articles in Macclesfield Courier, 1940-41.

Thomas, Nicholas, *Guide to Prehistoric England*, B. T. Batsford, 1960.

Toulson, Shirley, *Derbyshire, Exploring the Ancient Tracks*, Wildwood House Ltd., 1980.

de Tunstall Sneyd, Ralph, *Poems*, Wilfred Edmunds Ltd., 1929.

Ward, John, *The Borough of Stoke upon Trent*, original edtn. W. Lewis & Son, London, 1843; republished S. R. Publishers Ltd., 1969.

Ward, The Rev. R., *A Guide to the Peak of Derbyshire*, William Ward 1827 (reprint E. J. Morton, 1972).

Watkins, Alfred, *The Old Straight Track*, Methuen & Co. 1925 (reprint Garnstone Press, 1970, 1972, 1974 & 1980).

Westwood, Jennifer, *Albion, A Guide to Legendary Britain*, Granada Publishing and Book Club Associates, 1986.

We publish a wide range of titles, including general interest publications, guides to individual towns, and books for outdoor activities centred on walking and cycling in the great outdoors throughout England and Wales. This is a recent selection:

General interest:

THE INCREDIBLY BIASED BEER GUIDE – Ruth Herman
This is the most comprehensive guide to Britain's smaller breweries and the pubs where you can sample their products. Produced with the collaboration of the Small Independent Brewers' Association and including a half-price subscription to The Beer Lovers' Club. £6.95

DIAL 999 – EMERGENCY SERVICES IN ACTION – John Creighton
Re-live the excitement as fire engines rush to disasters. See dramatic rescues on land and sea. Read how the professionals keep a clear head and swing into action. £9.95

THE ALABAMA AFFAIR – David Hollett
This is an account of Britain's rôle in the American Civil War. Read how Merseyside dockyards supplied ships for the Confederate navy, thereby supporting the slave trade. The *Alabama* was the most famous of the 'Laird Rams', and was chased half way across the world before being sunk ignominiously. £9.95

PEAK DISTRICT DIARY – Roger Redfern
An evocative book, celebrating the glorious countryside of the Peak District. The book is based on Roger's popular column in *The Guardian* newspaper and is profusely illustrated with stunning photographs. £6.95

I REMAIN, YOUR SON JACK – J. C. Morten (edited by Sheila Morten)
A collection of almost 200 letters, as featured on BBC TV, telling the moving story of a young soldier in the First World War. Profusely illustrated with contemporary photographs. £8.95

FORGOTTEN DIVISIONS – John Fox
A unique account of the 1914 – 18 War, drawing on the experience of soldiers and civilians, from a Lancashire town and a Rhineland village. The book is well illustrated and contains many unique photographs. £9.95

ROAD SENSE – Doug Holland
A book for drivers with some experience, preparing them for an advanced driving test. The book introduces a recommended system of car control, based on that developed by the Police Driving School. Doug Holland is a highly qualified driving instructor, working with RoSPA. £5.95

Books of Walks:

RAMBLES IN NORTH WALES
– Roger Redfern

HERITAGE WALKS IN THE PEAK DISTRICT
– Clive Price

EAST CHESHIRE WALKS
– Graham Beech

WEST CHESHIRE WALKS
– Jen Darling

WEST PENNINE WALKS
– Mike Cresswell

STAFFORDSHIRE WALKS
– Les Lumsdon

NEWARK AND SHERWOOD RAMBLES
– Malcolm McKenzie

NORTH NOTTINGHAMSHIRE RAMBLES
– MAlcolm McKenzie

RAMBLES AROUND NOTTINGHAM & DERBY
– Keith Taylor

RAMBLES AROUND MANCHESTER
– Mike Cresswell

WESTERN LAKELAND RAMBLES
– Gordon Brown

WELSH WALKS:
Dolgellau and the Cambrian Coast
– Laurence Main and Morag Perrott

WELSH WALKS:
Aberystwyth and District
– Laurence Main and Morag Perrott

MOSTLY DOWNHILL:
Leisurely walks in the Lake District
– Alan Pears

WEST PENNINE WALKS
– Mike Cresswell

– all of the above books are currently £6.95 each

CHALLENGING WALKS IN NORTH-WEST BRITAIN
– Ron Astley *(£9.95)*

WALKING PEAKLAND TRACKWAYS
– Mike Cresswell *(£7.95)*Long-distance walks:

LONG-DISTANCE WALKS:

THE GREATER MANCHESTER BOUNDARY WALK
– Graham Phythian

THE THIRLMERE WAY
– Tim Cappelli

THE FURNESS TRAIL
– Tim Cappelli

THE MARCHES WAY
– Les Lumsdon

THE TWO ROSES WAY
– Peter Billington, Eric Slater, Bill Greenwood and Clive Edwards

THE RED ROSE WALK
– Tom Schofield

FROM WHARFEDALE TO WESTMORLAND:
Historical walks through the Yorkshire Dales
– Aline Watson

THE WEST YORKSHIRE WAY
– Nicholas Parrott

– all £6.95 each